Winning:
Living Your Best Life!

Howard Austin II

Winning: Living Your Best Life!

Copyright © 2019 by HOWARD AUSTIN II

All Rights Reserved.

No part of this publication may be reproduced in any form or by any means, including photocopying, scanning, recording, or otherwise without prior written permission of the copyright holder.

ISBN - 13: 978-1-7335829-0-2

Table of Contents

INTRODUCTION: Living Your Best Life: What does it mean? 7

CHAPTER ONE: Understanding Your Gift 11

CHAPTER TWO: Visions, Plans, and Goals 19

CHAPTER THREE: The Love Ingredient 31

CHAPTER FOUR: Building the Right Mindset 43

CHAPTER FIVE: Accept Responsibility 57

CHAPTER SIX: Be Innovative 73

CHAPTER SEVEN: Self-Discipline 79

CHAPTER EIGHT: Financial Excellence 91

CHAPTER NINE: True Goals of Life 97

CHAPTER TEN: Quotes and Scriptures 111

ABOUT THE AUTHOR 115

Acknowledgments

To my parents, Howard and Annette Austin

Thank you for being true examples of how to live one's best life. You have built your lives around making an impact, serving others and being a blessing to others. You have taught me so much, not only by the things that you have taught me but in the life that you have lived and continue to live. You have created an incredible legacy.

To my aunt, Donna

Like my mother, you have inspired me to know what true faith is. To look any obstacle right in the face and still have faith and praise no matter what. You have taught me to be resilient amid adversity. Thank you.

To my sister, Chrishawnta Austin-Perry

Thank you for being a great support to me. You have always encouraged me and looked out for me. I appreciate you.

To my grandparents, Howard J Austin Sr., Ernestine Austin, and Lottie Mae Evans

Thank you for being such awesome pioneers. Thank you for instilling the right values and leading your children and grandchildren along the right path. You have helped shape my life in a tremendous way.

Lastly, to the rest of my family and friends

Thank you for continuously supporting me and showing me true love. I appreciate you all!

Introduction

Living Your Best Life: What does it mean?

I believe Living Your Best Life means being all that you were created to be. It means becoming the best version of yourself and effectively walking in your purpose. It means doing the things that you were created to do! It means making your mark, it means making your impact!

I want you to know that you can start Living Your Best Life today.

You don't need to have it all together before you can start.

You don't need to have a full bank account to start Living Your Best Life.

You don't need to be in shape.

You don't need to have 10k+ followers on social media.

You need only to make the decision to start right where you are, because no matter where you are or what your situation might be, you can still live your best life—and better is to come!

> *The ultimate measure of a man is not where he stands during his moments of comfort and convenience. Rather, what does*

> *he believe in and what his course of action is during times of challenges and controversy. Achieving nothing worthwhile is easy but you have to cultivate an ability to overcome in unfavorable situations. Every unfavorable situation gifts you with the environment to demonstrate your true strength and determination for success. Always set your standards high, your greatest achievements lie within the infinite feats you achieve in your life. -**Martin Luther King Jr.***

In order to live your best life you need to be able to see beyond your present circumstance. How you view life determines whether you can live it to the fullest. You must also know that it is up to you whether this happens.

Living Your Best Life requires lots of hard work, courage, discipline, sacrifice and resiliency. It requires the ability to get back up after you've been knocked down. It's not about how far down you may have fallen, but it's about how far up you can bounce back and arise to higher and higher levels.

No one can stop you from Living Your Best Life—except you. And only you can make the decision to get started. It's on you to make it happen. So, make it happen! You have the power to do this. Everything that you need is already within you.

Living Your Best Life will give you ultimate satisfaction and joy because you will be doing the things you were created to do. You will experience feelings beyond your imagination! You will feel whole and complete, energized and enthusiastic!

The process of Living Your Best Life isn't so much about what happens around you, but rather it is about what's happening inside of you. It's about having joy that propels you every day. It is defined by continuous growth and a resilient spirit, the love you are able to give, your commitment and dedication to others, and the sacrifices you are willing to make.

To fully enjoy the benefits of a fruitful life, you must find joy within yourself. Never allow your circumstances to determine your self-esteem and happiness. Determine to be happy! You've got to make a pre-determined and conscientious decision in your mind to be happy.

It's up to us how we choose to react to situations. Many times, we naturally choose to react in a sad, agitated, argumentative, helpless, fearful, or combative manner to things that don't go our way, but just as we choose to allow ourselves to react and respond negatively, we can also decide to react positively. We have the power to decide to be happy—no matter what the situation may entail.

It starts today. It starts now. The process of becoming the best possible version of yourself will not necessarily be easy, but you can do it. The world is waiting for you to make your mark!

> *The way to get started is to quit talking and begin doing.*
> **-Walt Disney**

Your Mind

> *The most powerful tool in your life and in your body is your mind.* **-Bishop TD Jakes**

Do you have the mindset to live out your best life? Do you have the mindset to be blessed? Do you have the mindset for a break through?

You have to decide in your mind that you are going to live your best life, that you are going to be blessed! You have to make up in your mind that you will rejoice!

Psalm 118:24 tells us, *"This is the day that the Lord has made, I WILL rejoice and be glad in it."* You have to make the decision to rejoice. You have to say that I Will rejoice. I will live my best life. I will be blessed! I will achieve all that God has planned for me.

You have to make that decision and declare it.

As Bishop TD Jakes says, your mind is so strong. It is with the mind that we serve the Lord, and that is why the enemy fights you in your mind. The enemy doesn't have to tie you up with a rope for you to be bound. He ties you up in your mind with stress, worry, low self-esteem, pettiness, anger, fear, doubt, hostility, and rebellion. He can even make you physically sick if your mind is sick.

Proverbs 23:7 says "For as a man thinketh in his heart, so is he!" Determine in your mind and in your heart that you will live your best life!

So let's get with it!

Exercise

Note: Throughout this book, I have included exercises to help you apply the principles found here to your life. Answering these questions will help you reflect on the reading and lead you to Living Your Best Life. So, grab a journal and get started on your journey!

Write out the answers to the following:

- What does "Living Your Best Life" mean to you?
- Define success in your own words.

Chapter One

Understanding Your Gift

To live your best life, you must know that YOU ARE GIFTED! When God created you, He put gifts inside you. He tailor-made you! He knows everything about you. To live the best life that God intends for us, we must first identify our gifts and then seek to understand our purpose so that we can apply those gifts to fulfill our purpose.

We were all uniquely created and uniquely gifted to do great things! We have all been designed to do big things in our lives. In other words, we were all created to win.

You should know that your gift, when used in the way that God intended, will take you to great places. Proverbs 3:16 tells us that *"A man's gift makes room for him and brings him before great men"* (ESV), while 1 Peter 4:10 reminds us, *"As each has received a gift, use it to serve one another, as good stewards of God's varied grace"* (ESV).

At the beginning of the earth, God saw that His creation needed a physically present overseer. To solve that problem, God created you and me to rule over the Earth. Most importantly, we must remember that God made us in his own image. Just imagine the endless possibilities of that: we have infinite power and infinite abilities because we were made in the very likeness and image of God. We need to really understand the power that is inside of us. Sadly, many people choose to operate well below their potential throughout their lives, living beneath their "worth." You were created with greatness running through your veins!

> Then God said, "Let us make mankind in our image, in our likeness, so that they may rule over the fish in the sea and the birds in the sky, over the livestock and all the wild animals, and over all the creatures that move along the ground."
>
> So God created mankind in his own image, in the image of God he created them; male and female he created them.
>
> God blessed them and said to them, "Be fruitful and increase in number; fill the earth and subdue it. Rule over the fish in the sea and the birds in the sky and over every living creature that moves on the ground." - **Genesis 1: 26-28**

Exercise

- Write down your gifts, the things that you are uniquely good at and/or passionate about.
- Write down how you can better use those gifts to be more effective and how you can use them to be more impactful.

Understanding your Purpose

To live your best life, you must begin by understanding your purpose. Purpose can be defined in many ways, but its general meaning refers to doing what you were designed to do. Even though you are designed by God to have dominion, you are not created to do everything. There will be definite areas of strength, as well as areas where you will not fit in. Your job is to identify both and do that which is needful.

CHAPTER ONE: UNDERSTANDING YOUR GIFT

Understand that your true purpose is not to just serve yourself but to serve others. You are here to help make the world a better place.

Many people are trying to live out other people's purpose in life. For example, children may try to live out their parents' dreams instead of their own. Sometimes, we can get caught up trying to please or appease our parents, loved ones, or friends, forgetting that we have to live according to our own purpose and not anyone else's. Trying to live someone else's purpose and dreams will never bring you the joy that you crave, and you will never achieve complete satisfaction—regardless of how much external "success" or money you accumulate. Money, alone, will never equate to true fulfillment.

Seek to understand your purpose from the Creator, and then identify what you are good at and passionate about.

Those who live with the idea of doing everything to satisfy only themselves usually find out that they live unfulfilled lives. This is because we were never meant to be selfish in our purpose. The woman who keeps smiling as she gives out packages to the homeless may be achieving her purpose as she puts smiles on the faces of others and lives her best life in the process. The man, who devotes himself to teaching and coaching young boys to help guide them on the right path in life and provide mentorship and love that they might not ever know without him, can be living his best life. A beautician or barber working in a salon or starting his or her own shop, who has a passion for helping others look their best, can be walking in their purpose.

Walking in your purpose and Living Your Best Life is not about how much money you can make or how much fame or success you can accumulate. It is more about what you use your gifts and talents for, to help make things better. When you engage your gifts to satisfy yourself alone, you are not Living Your Best Life.

1 Corinthians 9:24 tells us, *"Don't you realize that in a race everyone runs, but only one person gets the prize? So, run to win!"* This scripture refers to the race of life, which leads to achieving eternal salvation. Most importantly, it tells us that we must run to win. This means that we can't just go through life walking aimlessly, without any clear purpose. We must run this race of life to win and gain the ultimate prize of salvation. We must race towards the objective of being the best version of ourselves and becoming the best that God intends for us to become.

Living our best lives isn't simply showing up or saying that we tried; rather, we should run to win! Let's strive to win the race of life, which is eternal salvation, as well as running towards achieving everything God has in store for us while here on Earth.

Run to win!

Define Your "Why"

To live your best life, you must have a reason for what is driving you to be your best. You must have a "why" behind what you are doing and what you are seeking to do. You must even have a "why" behind walking in your purpose. Think of it like this: your "why" is the reason you seek to change and become better. Your "why" may be your children, your spouse, or your parents. Your "why" is the reason you strive to be the best you can be. Your "why" may be that you want to grow in your relationship with God and study His word more, so you can better teach or be a greater example to your family. Your "why" may be to become a better athlete or a professional athlete and earn income to take care of your family. Your "why" may be that you want to become a teacher, doctor, lawyer, accountant, pastor, medical worker, or other professional to help others in a unique way. Your why may be to help people in their times of need or to inspire the next generation.

CHAPTER ONE: UNDERSTANDING YOUR GIFT

Your "why" is the reason that you are doing what you are doing. Your "why" is the component that is going to push you to be resilient, persistent, and consistent, even when you don't feel like doing what you need to do. When you feel like giving up, your "why" will keep pushing you forward. Another way to look at your "why" is to ask yourself, Why do I want to be my best? Why do I want to achieve this goal that I'm setting out to accomplish? Your answer will be your "why."

Exercise
- Identify your "why."
- Why do I want to be my best?

Dream

You have to know that everybody is not always going to agree with your dream. Everyone is not always going to support your dream. Everyone isn't always going to believe in your dream. But if God gave you the dream and the vision, that's all that really matters. It's on us to see those dreams through. We've got to have the faith that it will happen, put in the work to make it happen, and not ever quit or give up. If He gave you the dream and the vision, He's going to see it through. You just have to not give up. Most dreams don't come to pass, not because the person is incapable, but it's because they give up too quickly.

Understand that your walking in your vision and dream, will take time. At times, things will go wrong and you may even feel like you are so far away from arriving at your destination. But just keep pressing on and pushing forward. Wherever you are in life towards the pursuit of your dream, it's all happening for a purpose. Learn the lessons and stay focused and don't give up. You can live your dreams! You just have to not give up; you just have to keep the faith! You just have to be willing to do what it takes and make the necessary sacrifices that are required.

Is your dream big enough?

If you can accomplish the dream that you have in your heart all by yourself, your dream is too small. Your dream should rely upon God and involve locking arms with others to make it come true. You must be willing to do whatever it takes!

> *Dreams are for free, but hustle is sold separately* -**Mike Haman**

You have to be committed! You have to be consistent!

Ideas are a dime a dozen, but the execution is rare.

You can do it!

I'm reminded of the story of Joseph in the Bible. God gave him a dream. When he first told his brothers and father about the dream, they hated him, despised him and didn't believe his dream.

As a result they plotted against him and Joseph was then sold into slavery. He also ended up being imprisoned as well along his life's journey.

So looking at his story, it seems as if his dream would never come true. Imagine being Joseph. If God gave you a dream and then you were sold into slavery and then imprisoned, would you still have faith that your dreams would come to pass? For many of us, we would begin to doubt, give up, and lose faith.

Just as so many of us do nowadays, when we face adversity or rejection. We simply give up.

CHAPTER ONE: UNDERSTANDING YOUR GIFT

You may be trying to start a business for the dream that's been placed in you, but you can't seem to get financing and keep getting rejected by every lender. Or you may have a dream to be a licensed professional, but have failed your tests to become licensed. You may have a dream to be a producer, but you are currently homeless and living out of your car. We all will arrive at points in our lives where we think our dream is hopeless and will never become manifest. Where we feel our dream is impossible.

But keep the faith, because Joseph's story ended in his dream coming true. The things that he dreamt came to pass. And just as his dreams came to pass, so can ours, so can yours!

Chapter Two

Visions, Plans, and Goals

You Must Have a Vision

Vision is a glimpse of the future that God has purposed for you. If you don't allow yourself to gain a clear vision and perspective, you will rarely maximize your potential. To live your best life, you must have a vision for your life. You must tap into your creative nature and paint a picture in your mind as to what your life should actually look like. You must be able to know what you want your future to look like.

Many times, as we seek God and pray, He will give us different ideas and dreams, and we take those things in creating our vision. The vision is being able to forecast what things should look like or what they will look like eventually. It is part of your road map. It's a glimpse of the result or final product. You must not be afraid to have a GREAT vision that changes the world. Remember, we were placed here on this Earth for a purpose and we are all uniquely gifted, so with those things, it will begin to help create a vision for our life.

Don't be afraid to have a vision that impacts the WORLD!

As you are seeking guidance and defining what the vision is for your life, know that the vision may entail great successes, but the right vision also serves a purpose beyond just ourselves. For example, if your vision is to become President of the United States or CEO of a company, or whatever it may be, it must also include your "why," as well as how it will further help serve a purpose beyond just yourself and help advance the kingdom.

God gives great ideas, visions, and dreams. In doing so, we must make sure that our vision is in alignment with our purpose, one that will help serve and benefit others. God gives us great visions, not to just boast up ourselves, but to advance His kingdom.

The vision that you have for your life is very important. If you don't have any sort of vision or a lowly vision for yourself, then that low vision will be a guiding point to living your life, and if the vision for yourself is low, you won't strive to be all that God has created you to be. Your vision for your life should look like the very best of yourself. If you don't believe that your best is yet to come, or that you can do better, and that you can be Great, there is also little hope that your vision will manifest into anything meaningful.

As you have your vision, you must then also make sure you ENVISION yourself walking in that vision. You must take the time to sit back and see yourself living out that vision.

Ask yourself this question: If money were not an issue, what do you see yourself doing or becoming?

A true vision will always build others up rather than pull them down.

Exercise

- Write out the vision for your life
- Create a vision board

CHAPTER TWO: VISIONS, PLANS, AND GOALS

Know What You Believe In

Matthew 21:22 proclaims, *"If you believe, you will receive whatever you ask for in prayer."* Ephesians 3:20 tells us, *"Now to Him who is able to do exceedingly abundantly above all that we ask or think, according to the power that works in us."*

Do you truly believe in God and His power? What do you believe about yourself? Who do you believe God is? What do you believe He can perform?

All these questions are pertinent. Your answers to these questions will determine much, as you go about Living Your Best Life. If you can't believe in yourself, you won't ever be able to live your best life. Even if you believe in God but don't believe in your own capability, you still will only reach half your potential. Therefore, you need to not only increase your faith in God and His power but also increase your faith in yourself and in the abilities that He's put inside of you.

If you use what is placed inside of YOU, with His help and guidance, you can accomplish so many great things. You must believe in the greatness that has been placed within you. His word says in Ephesians 3:20, "Now to him who is able to do immeasurably more than all we ask or imagine, according to his power that is at work WITHIN US." So, believing in yourself is just as important as believing in God. God works through us, and we must have the faith and belief in ourselves that God can and does work through US to accomplish amazing things. Believe in yourself and in the source within you that is at work.

To live your best life, you must have an unwavering belief in your source, which is God, yourself, and what you're doing. You must believe, even when no one else does. You must believe, even when your current circumstances may not look like the desired result. When your bank account is zero or in the negative or when the doctor says there's no hope and you or your loved ones don't have long to live, you must believe. You must believe that your future is not defined by your current travails.

Your best days are still ahead!

Don't limit God with small expectations and small beliefs! God is bigger than anything you can ever imagine. *"His thoughts are not your thoughts; His ways are exceedingly above anything you could ever think or ask"* (Isaiah 55: 8-9).

Believe that better is in store. Know that what you believe will ultimately determine your expectations. If you don't believe in much or don't expect much, you won't get very much. In too many occasions, we have small and limiting beliefs. Sometimes we put God in a box, and this inhibits our ability to soar.

Don't limit yourself based on small beliefs in God and in yourself.

If you don't believe that you can be or have better, chances are you won't. If you don't believe that you can have your dream job or career, then there is a high chance that you won't ever get it. If you don't believe that miracles happen, that storms can be overcome and that God can provide, then you are limiting His power.

He has given us all GREAT power so that we can live our lives to the fullest, no matter what our current situations are. He has given us the brilliant minds that we can use to visualize, as well as the power in Him to achieve whatever output our minds come up with.

Your faith and belief in yourself is powered through your belief and faith in God and what He has said we are capable of doing through Him. It is not a belief or faith just based upon your own merit, but its based upon knowing who you were created by and what you were created to do . . . Great things!

CHAPTER TWO: VISIONS, PLANS, AND GOALS

Your belief also determines how much you're willing to fight. If you don't really believe in something, you won't really fight for it. But if you strongly believe in it, you'll fight to the end, even if some may tell you it's not possible. You've got to be willing to fight and put up a fight for the things that you believe in. Nothing is going to simply come easy or be handed to us. Believe in something that's worth fighting for. And don't be a quitter.

Don't give up simply because you have to fight. In every prize, in every race, it's a fight. For every prize, for every reward, there's a fight. There's a fight between good and evil. There's a fight between giving in to what is easy versus doing what is necessary. There will always be a fight.

While believing and having faith, you must also be willing to be adaptable. Sometimes our methods of reaching our goals may need to be adjusted or updated. So don't always remain stuck in your method; be adaptable when it calls for it. Just remember to never lose sight of your belief or the end goal. Be willing to fight for it and never forget to pray. Matthew 21:22 reminds us, "You can pray for anything, and if you have faith, you will receive it."

Believe that God is great, and then begin to act like it. To live your best life, you must accept the knowledge that GOD IS GREAT and remain in a constant fellowship with God so that He can show you the plans He has for you.

Plan

Every successful person always has a plan in the works. What is your current plan? Do you have a plan, or is it just a thought residing in your mind?

You must be intentional and detailed in your planning.

Here are a few things to remember about planning:

- Make intentional plans about your future.
- Break the plans into achievable milestones.
- Discard every form of vagueness and let your plan be very clear.
- Always be guided by your vision and purpose.
- Take time and brainstorm your thoughts and ideas.

It is vital to attach timelines to your goals, because deadlines and timelines help propel you towards achieving your goals.

There is a dream, a vision, and a purpose inside of you that the world is waiting for. Steve Jobs once said that the things we see all around us today are made up by people who are no smarter than you and me. So, take time to brainstorm, visualize, and imagine ideas to make the world a better place, and then set your plan in place to make it happen!

Set Goals

Discipline is the bridge between goals and accomplishment.
-Jim Rohn

Motivational speaker Brian Tracy once said, "Only three percent of adults have written goals, and everyone else works for them." This three percent earns more than all the other 97 percent put together. This is because the three percent already have clearly stated goals and the plans to achieve them. Doing so allows you to stay focused and helps to measure where you stand in the process towards achieving those goals.

Goals that are not written down are only hopes and wishes. Rather, take action by writing down your goals. Act on those goals and live

CHAPTER TWO: VISIONS, PLANS, AND GOALS

your best life. Even God commands us to always do so in Habakkuk 2:2: *"And the Lord answered me, Write the vision; make it plain on tablets, so he may run who reads it."*

Here are a few things to always remember when setting goals:

1. Make sure that your goals are specific, measurable and have a deadline.

This simply means that your goals should not be vague or general but need to be specific and in enough detail to be able to measure whether you are on pace to achieve the goal.

An example of an unspecific, unmeasurable goal with no deadline would be as follows:

I want to be financially independent and want to earn a lot more money.

An example of a specific, measurable goal with a deadline would be as follows:

I want to become financially independent by increasing my monthly income by $5k monthly by December 2019.

The above example provides the specific and measurable details with a deadline, so you can measure where you stand towards your goal and you have a clear target.

Goals that are specific, measurable, and have deadlines help give you a very clear target.

2. Your goals must be challenging but realistic.

Set goals that challenge you to rely on a source greater than just yourself. Les Brown says, "Most people fail in living out their potential in life, not because they aim too high and miss, but because they aim too low and they hit it." To live your best life, you must set challenging goals for yourself.

It is good to set an overall goal with a deadline. To help make your goal more attainable, you begin to also set milestones. A milestone is a benchmark towards your final goal. It's like setting a sub-goal along the journey towards your ending goal.

For instance, in the example mentioned earlier, we said that we want to become financially independent by increasing our monthly income by $5k by December 2019, and so we may create a milestone towards that main goal that says,

I will increase by monthly income by $2k monthly by April 2019, as a benchmark towards my overall goal of increasing my income by $5k by December 2019.

3. *Once you set your goals, create a plan as to how you are going to achieve your goals.*

Once the goals are set, you create your plan as to how you will go about making progress so that you achieve your end goal. For instance, if your goal is to increase your monthly income by $5k by December 2019, and you have a milestone of increasing your income by $2k by April 2019, you should begin to create a plan as to how you will go about increasing your income. I believe that you should first think about how you can feasibly meet your end goal. In this case, how you can possibly increase your income by $5k a month. Then as you identify ways of how you can possibly arrive at your end goal, then you begin to write out your immediate plan to accomplish either your first milestone or the goal itself. Think of all the ways you can generate an additional $5k a month, then put a plan in place as to how you will begin by creating the first additional $2k. Once you hit that goal, keep working your plan towards accomplishing that end goal.

Exercise

- Write down your goals and your plan to achieve them.
- List the goals that you have for yourself and your family. Make sure the goals are SMART (Specific, Measurable, Attainable, Realistic and Timely)

The Power of Today

Get up each day with the determination and motivation to WIN the day! Each new day is a day filled with so much opportunity, even if yesterday was tragic. Each new day is a day filled with another opportunity to carry out our purpose. That's ultimately why we are blessed to see a new day—it's another opportunity to make our mark on this world.

Each new day is filled with new opportunity, new hope, new favor, new grace, and a fresh chance to make progress. There is power in each day. Your best life can begin today! You make progress towards your goals by starting today. You can begin creating your plan today!

Life doesn't just happen to us. It's all about the decisions and choices we make and how we decide to respond to every situation. Your everyday choices determine your future. The change and improvements that you want to see start with making changes to your everyday habits.

To live your best life, take action. Start wherever you are. Each day take small steps towards your goals. Establish a strong work ethic and habits. Whatever you do repeatedly soon becomes a habit. Once a habit is formed, it is hard to break.

Each day is a new opportunity to be your very best! Determine that each day you arise, you will set out to make that day better than your last. So in a sense, it doesn't really matter if you failed or came up short yesterday, because if you determine that today day is going to be your best and take the steps to do that, then you have just made yourself better, regardless of what happened yesterday, or last week or last month, or last year. As you begin to change your habits and make improvements daily, you will begin to create victories for yourself and gain momentum. As a result, you continue to build upon that momentum and get better and better. But it all starts with Today! And what we chose to do today!

So make the most out each day! And wake up determined to WIN the day.

Daily habits

Each day you should get into the habit of creating a schedule and a plan for your day.

Set a schedule and begin to do things at a set time. Just as you have a schedule for work, create a schedule to incorporate other things that you need to accomplish on a daily basis. Build those things into a daily routine and habit.

For instance, if you want to read more, incorporate it into your schedule. Schedule to do it at a certain time each day. And dedicate that time to do so. Whatever you want to do, put it on a schedule and incorporate it into your habits.

The time to start is now. Don't put off for tomorrow what you can do today. Don't start someday. Start today!

CHAPTER TWO: VISIONS, PLANS, AND GOALS

If you do not begin to form great habits, you will never establish great habits tomorrow. The things we do today have an impact on our tomorrow, and we always have the power to make a positive impact.

What you do today, will shape your tomorrow.

Just look at your daily habits and they will indicate your tomorrows.

It's not your past that will shape your future, but it is rather what we do in the present. What we do with each day, determines our progress.

Exercise

- Commit to spend at least an extra hour a day, to move from average performance to superior performance.
- List the things that you will do in order to do so.

Studies show that usually after about 21 days doing things consecutively, habits are formed. Make a list of things that you will do for 21 days to help improve your habits.

Chapter Three

The Love Ingredient

*Teacher, which is the greatest commandment in the Law? Jesus replied: Love the Lord your God with all your heart with all your soul and with all your mind. This is the first and greatest commandment. And the second is like it: Love your neighbor as yourself. All the Law and Prophets hang on these two commandments. -**Matthew 22:36-39 (NIV)***

An essential part to Living Your Best Life is to love. Love God first and love Him even more than you love yourself. You must also love others. Love can't just be something you say or keep to yourself.

Love is an action.

When you love someone or something, you show it by expressing certain acts of kindness, thoughtfulness and finding ways to invest time into the things that you love.

If you love sports, you spend time watching your favorite team. You may even go to games or buy team gear. You tell others about your team and boast about how great it is. You may even keep up with team stats because of your desire to be actively involved.

You may have a favorite TV show or reality TV show and commit time each week to watch your favorite show and follow the TV star on social media and even support his or her product offerings.

The same should apply to your love for God and others. You should be actively involved and look forward to spending time with God as well as those you love. While it is important to tell God and to tell others that we love them, it is equally as important that we express our love in actionable ways. So just as we love to tell others about the details of the most recent TV episode or talk about the highlights from the show or season, we should love to tell others about our God and the good things He is doing in our lives and what He is able to do in the lives of others.

We should look forward to the next episode, chapter, and time to spend with God. We must also have that kind of love for others as well, and not just for the people who treat us well, but for all of mankind. We must ask ourselves this: Do my actions show my love for God? Do my actions show my love of others?

Spend Time With The Creator

It is important to develop a relationship with God, your Creator. Set aside some time to spend with Him consistently. Talk to Him—whether it be seeking guidance, a better understanding of your purpose, or whatever it is that may be on your heart. It's also important to take time to study the word of God and allow yourself to hear from Him.

It will be greatly beneficial to create a habit of spending at least fifteen to twenty minutes a day in prayer, reading His word, meditating, and hearing from Him. Of course, the more we grow in our relationship with Him, the more time we will want to spend with Him and dedicate to Him.

CHAPTER THREE: THE LOVE INGREDIENT

Make God your top priority, and He will open doors you could never imagine. Scripture says in Matthew 6:33, "Seek the Kingdom of God above all else and live righteously, and He will give you everything you need" (NIV).

Exercise

- Begin to create a daily habit of spending at least fifteen to twenty minutes a day in prayer, reading His word, meditating, and allowing yourself to hear from God.

Pray

> *Prayer moves the hands of the people that move the world.*
> **-Pastor Mike Haman**

In order to live your best life, incorporate the practice of prayer into your life. Make it a point to pray on a consistent basis. Build prayer into your life as a habit.

Make prayer a habit so that it becomes an automatic part of your life. Just like brushing your teeth every morning when you wake up, it should be an automatic habit. Incorporate prayer into your life in the same way so that it also becomes an automatic habit.

When you pray

Be authentic. Keep it real. You don't have to be polished. You just need to be real. The power is in being real. He already knows what you need; He wants you to be real enough to be real with Him. Don't put on a façade and pray to impress others by trying to use impressive words or big words—just be authentic and pray from a place of authenticity.

Don't always get so caught up in repetitious prayers that you have heard from others or that have been passed down.

While those memory prayers are great to put into our minds, we also must make sure that we are also praying what comes directly from our hearts and minds.

Part of being real is also being able to admit our shortcomings and asking Him for help where we need help, as well as asking Him for forgiveness for those things that we have done wrong. Just be real and keep it real with God!

It's only about one audience. It's about you talking to God. It's about you and Him.

Listen. When you pray, don't do all the talking. You need to listen. When you go to pray, bring the Bible. What we say to God is important, but what He has to say to us is even more important. We serve a living and talking God. So be sure that you allow the Lord to speak to you. Make sure that you seek to listen and not just do all the talking. When you pray, have your Bible nearby.

Have Faith.

Your breakthrough is connected to your belief—your faith.

In Mark 11:22-24, Jesus tells His disciples to *"Have faith in God. Truly, I say to you, whoever says to this mountain, 'Be taken up and thrown into the sea,' and does not doubt in his heart, but believes that what he says will come to pass, it will be done for him. Therefore, I tell you, whatever you ask in prayer, believe that you have received it, and it will be yours."* Hebrews 11:1 calls faith the *"confidence in what we hope for and assurance about what we do not see."*

"Truly I tell you, if you have faith as small as a mustard seed, you can say to this mountain, 'Move from here to there,' and it will move. Nothing will be impossible for you." – Matthew 17:20

CHAPTER THREE: THE LOVE INGREDIENT

In order to live your best life, you must have faith. Faith is defined as having complete trust and confidence in something or someone. What do you have faith in? Who do you place your faith in? In order to live your best life, you must know what you believe. On the journey of being the best that God wants us to be, we must know that our faith will be tested. Our professed beliefs will be tested.

You must define your faith and what you believe in.

To gain great clarity and build our faith even stronger, we must study the Word of God. We must know what God wants us to believe. To live your best life, you must increase your faith because your level of faith also helps determine your expectations of God!

Exercise

- Make a list of the things that you are believing God for.
- Pray about these things every day.

Trusting in God

In life, we will inevitably face troubles. And it is human nature to be afraid sometimes. We may be scared when we want to take a big step, and this fear may deter us from moving forward. In order to overcome this fear, it is important to establish a personal relationship with God and build your trust in Him. As you get to know Him more intimately, your trust and reliance on Him will increase.

As you develop your relationship with God, surround yourself with people who will pray with and for you. Find prayer partners because there is power in touching and agreement with others, as Matthew 18:19-20 tells us, *"I also tell you this: If two of you agree here on earth concerning anything you ask, my Father in heaven will do it for you. For where two or three gather together in my name, there am I with them."*

As you pray for yourself, also pray for your loved ones. Pray for others and their needs. Pray for people you don't know personally. Also, pray for those who plot against you and those who may have hurt you.

Intentional Joy

Those who live their best lives intentionally make up their mind to be happy and to be filled with joy! No matter your circumstances, you've got to be intentional about remaining positive and having joy. Know in your mind that there will be things that will try to steal your joy. There will be things that happen that will try to keep you down, leaving you feeling negative and hopeless. And since you already know this, you must make up your mind that you are going to stay even-tempered and continue to look up and smile.

Don't get discouraged and hold your head down. Be intentional in your decision to not let certain things steal your joy and get you bent out of shape. Those that live their best lives don't allow every little thing to bother them or steal their joy. Just because certain things may happen to you or certain things may be done to you or certain things may not go your way doesn't mean that you have to let them take your joy away. Rise above it and still be joyous!

In order to live your best life, you must have joy! And it doesn't just happen automatically. You've got to *intentionally* seek joy! Your Creator will give you ultimate joy!

> *A joyful heart is good medicine, but a crushed spirit dries up the bones.* -**Proverbs 17:22 (ESV)**

You can't live your best life with a sour attitude. You must commit time to activities that ultimately bring you joy and happiness, that are good-natured. Take time to enjoy yourself! In order to be your best self, you must able to BE your best self.

CHAPTER THREE: THE LOVE INGREDIENT

Be intentional about doing things that bring happiness. Make sure you intentionally incorporate good fun into your life. The key, however, is also using discernment and self-discipline in doing those things. For instance, if there are things that you want to do that bring happiness, such as shopping, traveling, or going to the spa, then you should do those things. However, you've also got to be sure to use discernment and discipline as to how often and how frequently you do these things.

Make sure that you incorporate your fun and happy things into your budget. Make sure that you aren't seeking happiness in a manner that's adversely impacting you. If you don't use discernment to do certain things the right way, things that could bring happiness can actually become hindrances.

The things that we should be intentional about are the things that we were created and purposed to do—what helps us to carry out our Father's business. They should be things that help build up the Kingdom of God, allow us to be of service to our fellow man, and show love.

Surround Yourself with the Right People

Those closest to you influence you in various ways. Therefore, you have to surround yourself with the right people and be wary of whose advice you take to heart. Nowadays, everyone has a platform for his or her voice to be heard. It's important to filter certain things because not everything that is shared and not every celebrity or known influencer should a positive influence on your life.

> *Find a group of people who challenge and inspire you, spend a lot of time with them and it will change your life.* -**Amy Poehler**

Research shows that you are likely to adapt to many of the behaviors of those who are closest to you, the ones that you spend the most time with. So if those around you are usually negative, always complaining, unmotivated, always looking for shortcuts, cutting corners, or looking to always lower the standard, you will likely eventually find yourself saying and doing the same types of things.

Conversely, if those around you are usually positive, looking to help and inspire others, spending time learning new skills and information, or reading valuable books and materials, then you are likely to adopt some of those same behaviors.

It's important that in Living Your Best Life you make it a point to be around some new people as well—people who have high-performance standards and bring new ideas. New people can inspire you to elevate yourself. Expand your peer group to include people who have greater knowledge, greater expertise, and greater success than you do.

Make it a point to spend more time with these people. Always look to expand your circle of friends and colleagues that can have a positive influence on you. Value your current positive and valuable relationships, and look to expand.

Don't be afraid to surround yourself with people who are more knowledgeable than you on certain things. These people will challenge you to raise your standards and propel you towards the next level in your chosen career or area of focus. Be willing to expose yourself to new knowledge and ideas. Meet new people who will positively impact your life. Be a part of a mentor group or create one yourself. In Living Your Best Life, you must make it a point to be around people that can help bring out the best in you.

Let me quickly show you some of the rudiments of choosing the right people because the quality of your team will determine the quality of your life. According to Brian Tracy, your choice of a "reference group" can help determine as much as 95 percent of your success and achievement. So, what are some indicators of a great reference group and team?

- The right people always find ways to positively reinforce good things.
- They are positive in their attitude and mentality.
- They help encourage you to be the best that you can be.
- They help raise the standard.
- They don't look to just settle nor let you settle.
- They help expose you to new things.
- They are willing to tell you the hard truth, in a positive manner, even if it the hard truth may to hurt your feelings.

Exercise

- List the names of the 5-7 people closest to you.
- List the names of those people that you really know should not be part of your group.
- Make a list of people you need to get to know as well as groups you need to become involved in.

Write out how you believe each person adds value to your life. If any of these people closest to you does not currently add value to your life, you need to reconsider their purpose in your life. Then decide whether you need to continue committing as much time to them as you currently are or make some modifications.

For those who positively impact you, make it a point to spend more time with them. For those who negatively impact you or simply don't add value to you, make it a point to spend less of your time with them.

Please note that this doesn't mean that any of the people who don't add value are bad people. You simply need to limit the amount of time you spend with them. This is important if you want to be more effective and make this your best year yet!

Judgment

In order to live your best life, don't be judgmental. Currently, we all seem to be so quick with our opinions. Everyone is entitled to his/her own opinion but, in the end, they are just that, opinions. So many things are now set before the court of public opinion.

It also seems that often times everyone wants to decide what is right or wrong for the next person, what should be decided about someone else, or how people should be perceived. We are so quick to judge and condemn people and situations. But in living our best life we don't look to be the judge of others. There's so many of us that want to cast stones against others, as if we ourselves have always been 100% perfect. We all have done some things that weren't right. We have all had slip-ups.

It's not our job to judge and determine the verdict for everybody else.

It is our job to help inform others, to help provide truth, to be the light and to make sure others are aware of what is right. It's our job to help provide information to become better and to grow. It's our job to help and to show love, and be an example, not to condemn. We have so many wanting to judge but not enough willing to help.

You aren't here to be a harsh critic and be judgmental; you are here to show love, mercy, and kindness. And as we do, we also reap those things in return. Sometimes, if we knew what people had been through, their sorrow and their suffering, maybe we would not be so quick to judge. Jesus tells us to get our own lives sorted out first. We are to change ourselves first before we try and change other people. See Matthew 7:1-5.

Instead of being so quick to judge, seek to understand. Imagine yourself in the other person's situation. Imagine if the shoe were on the other foot. How would you want others to handle the situation if the script were flipped? Think about that before you rush to judgment and run to criticize.

If you have an issue or a criticism, look to solve that problem discreetly. Look to resolve the problem through the proper channels. Don't just go run to the court of public opinion and run to social media and aim to "put everybody" on blast. First look to resolve your situation discreetly.

While we should be advocates and stand up for justice, we should not seek to be judgmental.

Chapter Four

Building the Right Mindset

*Your attitude, not your aptitude, will determine your altitude. -***Zig Ziglar**

According to Confucius, the man who thinks he can and the man who thinks he can't are both right. Think about that for a minute.

That's why it's so important that we make sure we adopt the right mindset. Having the right mindset is key to Living Your Best Life. It's one of the key components to achieving your dreams and goals.

In your mind you must also know that life won't always be crystal clear and 100 percent easy, you've got to know that adversity will come, as it is a part of life. No one has ever walked this earth without adversity. We all will have adversity. Even Jesus, the most perfect person ever to walk the Earth, was challenged with adversity. So, know that problems will come; no one will go without facing problems. But with the right mindset, you will be able to overcome and live your best life, even despite adversity.

Living Your Best Life involves a mindset of continuous growth and improvement. You've got to know that you can overcome whatever challenge comes your way. Also, know that the bigger your adversity, the sweeter the victory and greater the achievement once you overcome it!

Your expectations set the limits for your life.

If you expect little, you're going to receive little. If you don't anticipate that things can and will get better, they won't. But if you expect favor and favorable outcomes and keep the correct perspective, you shall receive.

Living Your Best Life doesn't mean your life will be free of problems. Expect to encounter various battles that must be won. However, you've got to know and trust your creator. Know that ALL things are possible, but you must also adopt a mindset that doesn't expect things to simply be handed over without a fight. So, prepare yourself to fight for your victory.

The journey to the top is filled with many diversions and problems. If it were not, everyone would reach his or her destination free from adversity. But know that God has prepared you. To live out your best, you need faith, fight, trust, hard work, discipline, resiliency, and perseverance.

In living our best life, we understand that we are not immune to everything and will face setbacks, trials, and challenges. As challenges are not always self-inflicted, but every challenge can build us up, if we have the proper perspective. Understand that there is purpose in every challenge or failure. Most people think challenges happen for no reason or are simply just bad luck and fail to learn from them. You must avoid this pitfall by always learning from your challenges, learning from trying times. Don't just go through experiences, learn from them. Use your experiences and your situations as opportunities to learn. Use the experiences to grow and become a better person.

Understand that God will never put more on you than you can bear. As scripture says in James 1:2-4, *"Dear brothers and sisters, when troubles of any kind come your way, consider it an opportunity for great joy."* For you know that when your faith is tested, your endurance has a chance to grow. So let it grow, for when your endurance is fully developed, you will be perfect and complete, needing nothing. The ability to learn from mistakes, sufferings and trouble should become ingrained in you. See your challenges as opportunities to grow and become a better person.

Another thing to understand is that going through certain terrible situations will make us more relatable. It gives us a better ability to help others who may go through a similar situation. We are given greater credibility because we have been there. When we acquire this "street cred," we can counsel others through their situations.

Attention to Detail

> *If you are going to achieve excellence in big things, you develop the habit in little matters. Excellence is not an exception, it is a prevailing attitude.* **-Colin Powell**

To live your best life, you must pay attention to the details. The small details make the big differences. It is important that you do not look for ways to cut corners. There's a difference between sweating the small stuff and paying attention to the small details. To me, sweating the small stuff means that you pay attention and give precedent to small things that have little or no value. To me the small "stuff" are things that are non-valuable and non-impactful to you or the bottom line. Things such as gossip, thing such as doubters, haters, things such as critics, things that don't really attribute to the bottom line.

Paying attention to the small details to me means, paying attention to the small things that have value, that are valuable. Making sure that the follow up call is placed to check on your most recent customer. Paying attention to the small details is following through on the things that you said you were going to have done. If you said you were going to send an email/text to someone and provide them a recommendation, it means you do just that and follow through on those small details that have value. One of the biggest factors in being set apart, is paying attention the small details and doing the small things that matter. Make it a point to master the small details and you'll begin to make big differences.

The Necessity of Sacrifice

In order to live your best life, you've got to be willing to not only give but to also give up certain things. You've got to be willing to sacrifice. Sacrifice your time. Sacrifice your energy. Sacrifice your convenience. Sacrifice your money.

Sacrifice for others, serve others. Give up your time to help others.

But also know that what do you do in secret God will reward in public

You've got to sacrifice in your work/profession, and do more than just what your paid to do. Do more than just 40 hours a week. Wherever there is a need be willing to fill it. Whether you are paid to do it or not. If you just keep finding ways to serve and filling the needs of others, you will be rewarded. God will reward you.

Sacrifice your comfort for the betterment of others and for the betterment of yourself and you'll experience breakthrough!

We all have to be willing to sacrifice or give up something that is dear to us. It all started with the great sacrifice that God made by sacrificing

His only son, Jesus Christ, who died for us and our sins so that we may have life and have it more abundantly. God Himself made the greatest sacrifice, so we, too, must sacrifice something great in order to live our best life.

The Necessity of Forgiveness

Be willing to forgive and let things go. We can't hold on to resentment forever; it only harms us. It keeps us bitter and has a negative impact on our health.

Resentment never allows us to move on.

It's also important to forgive and not live in a state of retaliation. Don't try to find ways to retaliate and pay others back that have done you wrong or offended you. Even though, its so much easier said than done, we must be willing to forgive those that hurt us and do us wrong and not look to retaliate against them.

It is essential that we all continue to grow in forgiveness, as this is usually one of the toughest areas for us all—to truly forgive. As it can be a hard, unnatural thing to do. Don't try to get back at or get even with others; learn to just give it to God. As He sees all and knows all, and He will take vengeance for you. But it's not for us to take revenge into our own hands.

Scripture tells us in Romans 12:17-19, *"Never pay back evil with more evil. Do things in such a way that everyone can see you are honorable. Do all that you can to live in peace with everyone. Dear friends, don't take revenge. Leave that to the righteous anger of God."* For the scriptures say in Deuteronomy 32:35, *"I will take revenge; I will pay them back says the Lord."*

The Necessity of Confidence

It is pertinent that you learn to value yourself in order to reach your full potential. If there is no personal belief in your own capabilities, there is absolutely no need to even try to engage in any pursuit in life. You should always strive to adopt a kind of confidence that is derived from knowing your Source. You are created in God's own image. Truly knowing this gives you all the confidence to surge ahead in all aspects of life.

You should have the utmost confidence in God and His word, what He says about you, what He put inside of you, and the great things that He can do through YOU!

While being confident, we must also still remain humble. We must remain approachable, teachable, and relatable. Being humble means not thinking of yourself as being untouchable or too good for something or that nothing can exist without YOU. In being humble you understand that you are who you are only because of the Source that works within you.

Use your Setbacks for Good

You must use your setbacks to help you become stronger and wiser. With the right perspective, you can become better as a result of your setbacks. When we are faced with setbacks, if we respond with the right attitude and mindset, we can become more resilient, more patient, more loving, more compassionate, more empathetic, and more focused.

You must understand that some of your setbacks are not just a test or experience that you go through just for yourself. Our setbacks and experiences we go through can also be opportunities for us to be able to relate to others and able to encourage others. With the right

CHAPTER FOUR: BUILDING THE RIGHT MINDSET

mindset, you trust God, and know that there is nothing too hard or difficult that you cannot overcome.

If God allowed it to happen, know that He allowed it to happen for a reason and He will never put more on us than we can bear.

So even though there will be pain, even though there will be tears and struggles because of some of the setbacks and challenges that we will face, know that if He allowed it to happen, it was for a reason. It's our job to make sure that we open ourselves up to listen, to reflect and allow Him to reveal the purpose and the lesson. The pain will be real. But many of times the setback, in conjunction with having the right mindset, becomes a driving factor in your betterment.

There are certain persons that have been victims to certain crimes and while of course our hearts go out to them and we wish those experiences never happened, but sometimes as a result of the setback or pain that did occur they use that pain and negative experience to become advocates and help others so that the same experience they went through others don't have to go through. That is how a tragic situation can still have good within it.

That dark situation can be a driving force to help create change in the world and help impact so many other people and their futures. Use your setbacks to become better! Things won't always be fun, nor easy, and can be hurtful and painful, but determine in your mind that you will be victorious. Determine that when it is all said and done, you are going to use your setbacks as something that will make you better, and help others as a result.

Falsely Accused / Being Imprisoned

Sometimes, in doing the right thing or good things, you can still be falsely accused and falsely imprisoned. Sometimes, doing good deeds doesn't mean that the immediate result will always feel "good." But you must know that if He does allow it to happen, it's part of his master plan. He has orchestrated or allowed it to happen for a purpose. Your job is to remain steadfast in trusting and believing in His word, and continue to plant good seeds, seeking to learn the lessons within the situation. Know that when you're doing what you're supposed to do—planting and sowing good seeds—negative things may continue to happen around you. Know that it's part of His purpose and He's going to bring you out stronger and better than ever in the end! You are going to get the victory!

There are many examples that come directly from the Bible that illustrate this concept. One such example is the story of Shadrach, Meshach, and Abednego found in the third book of Daniel. They were three Hebrew boys who did the right thing. They refused to bow down and worship a golden statue of a king over their Lord God. They did what many of us may be afraid to do. They made the tough decision to do what was right and not worship any other gods before their God. As a result of doing what was right, the immediate result was that they were thrown into a fiery furnace that was turned up seven times hotter than usual—so hot that it killed the guards who put them into the furnace. But in the end, God showed up right there in the midst, and they had the ultimate victory!

In Genesis, Joseph told his brothers of a dream that the Lord gave to him that allowed him to see his future. When he shared the dream that was given to him from above, he was then betrayed by his own brothers and sold into slavery. The immediate result of sharing his God-given dream was devastating, betrayed by his own brothers. But God orchestrated the situation and allowed him to eventually be put in a position of power/responsibility within Pharaohs' palace under a man named Potiphar, who was the head official to the King. Joseph became the highest person of responsibility in Potiphar's home.

CHAPTER FOUR: BUILDING THE RIGHT MINDSET

Joseph was then falsely accused by Potiphar's wife though she was the one who made advances towards him. Joseph chose not to give in to her advances and, in fact, ran away from her, and she accused him of false accusations, and he was thrown into prison. For Joseph, the immediate result of doing what was right was imprisonment.

However, while in prison he still gained favor. God allowed him to be imprisoned so that he could help others and use his gift of being able to interpret dreams. His gift allowed him to be able to interpret the dreams of the King himself. Consequently, the King made him governor of all of Egypt. He went from being enslaved to being imprisoned falsely to become the governor and the highest-ranking official in all the land next to the King. Then, he was also able to bless his family and the same brothers who sold him into slavery.

In Living Your Best Life, you come to understand that certain storms will come even when you are doing good. In both the good and bad times, know that He's in control and find the valuable lesson that you need to learn. As you realize the lessons to be learned, you will realize that the bigger the problem, the greater the glory God will get when He sees you through. God will show His omnipotent power.

In Living Your Best Life, you understand you will have some battles, but you will begin to understand that your blessings far outweigh your battles.

Mistakes Happen!

You will make some mistakes in life. We all are imperfect and will get some things wrong at some point in our lives. The key however is to not let your past mistakes hold you back from Living Your Best Life today or from your future. We all make mistakes but those living their best lives learn from their mistakes and keep moving forward.

We aren't perfect, so don't spend too much time sulking over your mistakes that you don't allow yourself to live in the present and learn from your mistakes. You can't be your best today, and you can't be your best in the future by constantly staying and living in your past. Ask for forgiveness, draw the lesson, and then move on.

You must also know that there will be certain people that will try and use your past mistakes against you. They may say that you will always be a certain kind of way, or that you will always be the person of your past. However, you cannot fall into that trap, of allowing your past to determine your present and your future. What happened years ago, months ago, weeks ago, or even yesterday, doesn't mean that the same thing has to happen today and tomorrow. Don't define or devalue yourself by the mistakes that you have made. Rather, allow those mistakes to be building blocks for your future.

Exercises

- Write down things that have been setbacks in your life
- Write down a list of things you have failed at
- Write down the lesson(s) you have you learned from these setbacks or failures
- Write down how you can use your setback or failure to help someone else

Understand the Value of Time

It is pertinent to understand the importance of your time. Time is valuable and how you spend it and who you spend it on and who you spend it with is very important. If you spend most of it on people who don't add value to you, or on activities that are invaluable, then you're wasting time. You must use your time wisely and spend it with people or things that add value.

We all have the same 24 hours in a day. Where the difference lies for those that are successful and those that aren't, is in how you spend your time.

Influencing Others

We are all influencers. How are you influencing those around you? Are you positively or negatively influencing those around you? What are others gaining from being around you? Are your personal social media pages only all about self-gratification? Are you using your platform to help be an example and to give life to others? Are you finding ways to not only just promote yourself, but also to give something to others for their betterment?

Remember that Living Your Best Life requires you to positively influence those around you. It requires you to help and make things better for someone else.

Exercise

- Write down how you are influencing those around you.
- If you aren't positively influencing those around you, write down how you will begin to do so.

The Growth Mindset

Growth doesn't happen by staying in your comfort zone. Rather, everyone who has encountered exponential success has had to leave his/her comfort areas to explore. A growth mindset allows you to learn from both your accomplishments and your failures and understands the need for personal reflection.

As you succeed, set aside time to reflect on what helped you achieve your goals. As you fail, set aside time to reflect on what went wrong and how things can be done differently moving forward. Look at how you can further build upon things that are working well or which have yielded desired outcomes.

To adopt a growth mindset, you need to always be seeking wisdom. To gain wisdom, you need to be a great listener. In a world where we are so quick to voice our opinions, the ability to listen has become even more valuable. Don't get caught up in always having to have something to say. Instead, listen, observe, and learn so you can have the most effective response to every challenge that confronts you and have the most effective response in meeting the need at hand. If you spend all of the time talking, you might miss great opportunities to better learn and understand.

You must know that you can't become who you were designed to be by remaining where you currently are. In other words, you can't go to the next level and live your best life by simply maintaining your current skill set and knowledge base. You must take constant action towards your growth, as growing is an active activity, not passive, activity.

The enemy of growth is comfort!

Some people are actually reducing their earning ability each year by not upgrading their skill set and knowledge. Whatever knowledge and skills you have today will soon become obsolete tomorrow, as there's always new information, technology, and regulations that are created or put in place. If you aren't continuously increasing your knowledge and skills, you'll be in danger of becoming ineffective.

For example, if I am a doctor and care for my patients but don't know how to integrate an electronic charting system into my office, then I may soon become ineffective when there is a shift and a mandate towards computer-based medical record keeping.

CHAPTER FOUR: BUILDING THE RIGHT MINDSET

People who don't continually re-invent themselves generally end up ineffective, even though they may possess great talents and skills.

In another scenario, if I have been a Marketing Director for many years and only know one way of marketing, traditional face-to-face marketing, my agency may soon become obsolete or experience a decline in sales because I have not taken time to constantly improve myself and my skillsets and learned newer marketing strategies and techniques such as digital marketing skills. If I don't do so, in this digital age that we are living in, I will soon become obsolete.

The same principle applies to us all, in our various careers and professions. You must take time to further learn and study your craft. Identify different training workshops, conferences, or materials that are related to your craft or passions and continually expose yourself to new information and materials and learn it.

Are you in tune with what's coming down the pipeline? And are you willing to reinvent yourself?

Exercise

- Begin to Invest three percent of your income in making yourself more valuable
- Create your training plan

Identify which trainings and conferences you will attend, which books, materials, and resources that you will purchase to help you become more knowledgeable and educated about your craft and industry.

Chapter Five

Accept Responsibility

It is nearly impossible to grow in any significant way when you don't take responsibility for yourself and your life. -**John Maxwell**

Accepting responsibility for your life is one of the most essential elements in Living Your Best Life because you can't live life to your maximum potential playing the blame game. There are too many examples today in our society of those who continuously fail to take responsibility for their actions.

For example, people will request extra-hot coffee and carelessly spill it on themselves, then they sue the establishment. Some will climb on top of a ladder and lean too far over, despite the warning labels on the product. When they fall, they will still look to find a way to sue the manufacturer for their injury.

When you continue to look to blame someone else for your past or for your bad choices or even your current predicament, your ability to live your best life is tampered with. Be willing to accept responsibility for your actions without always having to find someone to blame. You take responsibility.

It's your life and you must take responsibility.

You also have to let go of certain things that may have happened to you in the past, which you indeed may have had no control over. In those situations, it's your responsibility to determine how you respond to what happened and do so in a way that allows you to make progress.

It is your responsibility to live your best life and not let anything have ultimate power over you or the life God has set for you.

Exercise

Write down a list of things that you are responsible for in your life.

List the things you need to begin to take responsibility for right now.

No Excuses

Losers make excuses. Winners make progress.

Don't use your incredible brain to come up with excuses for not taking certain action. Either decide to do it or decide not to do it! It's as simple as that. Decide one way or the other and then act.

Develop and cultivate an attitude of no excuses.

It is sadly quite common to find that most people come up with many reasons why something cannot be achieved. They come up with all kinds of reasons why they can't be successful, why they can't make improvements, why they can't be victorious, and why they are destined to fail.

You should adopt a higher mentality if you want to succeed in life and spend your time focusing on all the reasons why you can and will be successful. Even if it's only one reason, focus on that one reason! Don't

CHAPTER FIVE: ACCEPT RESPONSIBILITY

fall into the trap of looking to identify a "legitimate or reasonable" excuse.

Know that those who are successful also don't feel like doing many of the same things that unsuccessful people don't feel like doing.

Those who are successful and maximize themselves also face challenges that they must conquer and overcome in order to be successful. Those who are successful have many of the same "excuses" as everybody else. However, they resolve in their mind and determine by their actions that they are not going to settle in letting the excuse defeat them. If you keep on giving excuses, don't wonder why you aren't successful—know that it's your excuses holding you back.

Successful people love to step out of the norm and take calculated risks that transition them to the top.

If you spend the majority of your time and energy focusing on how to make progress and how to create solutions and solve your problems and obstacles, as opposed to focusing the majority of your time on all of the reasons or excuses as to why you aren't or can't be successful, you'll make so much more leeway. Remember that we ALL can come up with all the reasons why something can't be done or why things aren't going to work out. That's easy and everybody is already doing that! But it is those who are set apart, that always focus on finding the solutions! They find the one reason why and how it can be done, when others say it can't be done.

Focus on finding solutions of how you are going to make it happen. Find a way!

Identify a need and then get started right there. Start making your impact wherever there is a need. Don't just complain about what's not happening. Start making things happen!

Decisiveness

In Living Your Best Life, you must be decisive. You have to be able to make a decision. Nothing is accomplished until a decision is made. Indecision keeps you stuck; it keeps you right where you are! Everything starts with a decision.

In arriving at decisions, we should be sure that we do the following:

- Seek wisdom and discernment from above to be guided in the right direction
- Conduct your own due diligence and research, study, and learn what needs to be learned to be informed
- Be open to receive feedback and insight from others.

Then you must take all the information and act by making a decision!

Anything can happen, and anything is possible based upon the power of a decision. Deciding to do something and/or deciding to stop doing something only happens if we are capable of making the decision.

In being decisive, you must always be willing to learn from your decisions. Not every decision that we make will be 100% correct. It's in those times that we must humble ourselves and allow ourselves to learn from decisions that didn't yield the best results. But the beauty of a poor decision is that a decision was actually made and since it was made, now you can gain greater wisdom and insight and now know more about how to handle the situation/decision next time, which makes you that much more knowledgeable. The decision that you made was what enabled you to gain greater understanding, wisdom, and insight.

CHAPTER FIVE: ACCEPT RESPONSIBILITY

Applying the Law of Focus

The Law of Focus says that you must be mindful of what you focus on. Don't let minor events distract you from the big picture. If you focus too much on the minor things, things that have no value, you will get off the course of prioritizing what is most important. And The Law of Concentration says that whatever you dwell on grows and increases in your mind. So it is very important that you focus on important things, focus on the right things and understand that not everything deserves your attention.

What we focus on determines our fruitfulness. If you want to be successful, you must be sure to focus on the right things. Focus on the things that are going to help you grow and add value to your life. Focus on the things that are going to help you be successful.

We should focus on the things from above and the things of God (Philippians 4:8). It's also important to focus on the things that are necessary to help you grow in knowledge and which will enable you to enhance your level of understanding of your craft. What I'm saying is, you can be passionate about something, such as having your own business or passionate about being a better leader or manager, or passionate about becoming a fitness expert, but if you don't also take time to learn and study things that will help you become more knowledgeable of how to run a business, or learn about the body and nutrition, then you may not be fruitful or successful because you don't spend enough time focusing on the things that are necessary to become more successful.

If you're spending all your time browsing and scrolling through gossip sites, shopping all the time for things that have no value, or focusing on what everyone else is doing, then you will not be able to focus on the necessary things that will bring you success in your life.

The Law of Focus also applies to positivity and negativity as well. You can't focus on negative things and expect to bear positive results and positive energy. It's hard to be both positive and negative at the same time. Make the decision to focus your mind, energy, and efforts on the positive productive things.

Focus and meditate on good things—the things that help make you better such as

- God's Word
- Learning your craft
- Identifying solutions and answers to problems
- How you can make things better
- How you can help others

> *"But whose delight is in the law of the Lord, and who meditates on his law day and night. That person is like a tree planted by streams of water, which yields its fruit in season and whose leaf does not wither—whatever they do prospers."* -**Psalm 1:2-3: (NIV)**

Eliminate Distractions

In order to stay focused you must be willing to eliminate certain distractions. It requires you having to say No to certain things.

There are many distractions that we can be sidetracked by, that adversely impact our ability to stay focused on the priority. You will need to look at the following areas and determine whether you need to eliminate or restrict certain distractions that are non-productive.

Are you saying Yes to too many things?

CHAPTER FIVE: ACCEPT RESPONSIBILITY

You cannot say YES to everything and still be able to focus on the things that need to get done. Sometimes you've got to say No to certain things. Sometimes you've got to say No to certain things until you can finish the things of priority that are presently before you. You can't always say Yes to every opportunity. Sometimes taking on too much or too many things or projects makes you less effective and doesn't allow you to remain sharp and focused on the things of greatest priority.

In saying that, you must learn to prioritize what is most important in order to stay focused and be most effective. You should always prioritize things by what has the greatest level of impact/value if it is done or not done. Meaning that if something has a huge impact if it isn't done or completed, those are the things that you need to prioritize first.

Sometimes we may get caught up in doing the things that are easy and putting off the things that are of most importance. However, it's important to prioritize what you focus your attention on based upon the value of importance, as well as the timelines or deadlines that are associated with it.

Are you spending too much time on your cell phone, the Internet, watching TV or just hanging out having fun all the time?

In order to live your best life, you've got to be willing to sacrifice some things. You must be willing to limit your exposure to certain things so that you can stay on track and stay focused. While we all love to incorporate fun into our habits, which we rightfully should do, we can't have our habits and routines to only be about doing what is easy and fun and overly consumed with certain things.

Spending too much time on your phone, or on social media, is often one of the biggest distractions today that needs to be eliminated or restricted. You must restrict your amount of exposure to these things.

Every minute that you spend doing things that are not of priority, takes you away from making progress. If you eliminate certain distractions you'll begin to spend much more of your time in a more effective way, making progress and getting closer and closer to your goals. Understand that the habits you currently have will largely determine your tomorrow.

You succeed when you do what it takes to be effective and then do those things over and over until those behaviors become your habits.

Making the Tough Call

You must be willing to make tough decisions in order to live your best life! Many times, we must make certain tough decisions that may hurt to be our best. Sometimes those tough decisions may be having to move on from certain toxic environments or relationships. Sometimes those tough decisions may include having to stand up for what you believe in and go against the grain, in speaking your truth to those that you love and care about, even if it may disappoint or upset.

Sometimes those tough decisions may include not putting yourself in certain environments that you may "like" or that feel good to you, but you know that they are potentially harmful for you in the end. Sometimes the tough decision may include having to say no to something that may give you great financial reward, but if it's at the cost or expense of losing certain other things, compromising your values, or having to sacrifice who you are or what you believe in, you may be faced with making such tough decisions. Sometimes it may be having to accept that you need help and making the tough decision to seek help or treatment.

As we go about striving to grow, we must know that Growth itself requires you to not only make a decision but often requires certain tough decisions in order to grow.

CHAPTER FIVE: ACCEPT RESPONSIBILITY

For example, sometimes you may be spending too much time with people that you care deeply about but are adding no value to you. You may have to make a difficult decision to distance yourself and not spend as much time with them.

Sometimes we've got to make a tough decision to leave a relationship that we know isn't for us and, in the long run, isn't in our best interest. Sometimes we must make the tough decision to let certain people go at work. The person may be a nice and pleasant person to be around, but if he or she isn't adding value and is continuously hurting the team, then you've got to be willing to make certain tough decisions.

Sometimes you've got to make tough decisions to leave a job or to turn down an opportunity that you know isn't best for you. You've got to make those tough decisions that go against what's popular.

Nothing great has ever been accomplished without making some tough decisions!

Think about God and how He made a tough decision to send His only begotten Son into the world to die for our sins! That's a tough decision!

Think about Jesus who had so many tough decisions He had to make, including making the decision to love those who betrayed and doubted him. He made the tough decision to pay the ultimate sacrifice and become crucified for our sins so that we could be cleansed and forgiven.

Jesus was faced with many tough decisions that had to be made. He even asked God to take the cup of suffering away. But He ultimately made the tough decision to allow God's will to be done and decided to sacrifice His Life for you and me.

Living our best life requires us to make tough decisions! Know that it won't always be easy but that it's your responsibility and duty to make the necessary tough decisions to be your best!

Who Said Life Was Supposed to be Easy?

Life was never created to be easy. Come to this realization.

You were created for this life in order to mature, to grow, to serve, to love, to make an impact and to be all that you were created to be. And none of those things are easy. Growth is neither easy nor convenient. Maturation takes time, requires patience and resiliency and requires you to go through some hard things. In serving, it requires putting the needs of others before your own needs. To love requires forgiving and forgiveness. None of these things are easy, just as life is not easy.

We must realize that life is full of tests and challenges. Life is full of adversity. Life is full of resistance. Life is a challenge!

But it is designed so that in the end, you become better!

Don't look for everything to be easy. Instead be ready and willing to face the challenge! Embrace the challenge! The greater the test, the greater the challenge, the greater the victory! Stop focusing on things being hard, as life's not supposed to be easy. So spend your time focusing on how you will respond and overcome the challenges at hand.

Become a Person of Your Word

Be timely: You must make sure your word means something and this means you should deliver according to the time that you promise. In the workplace, church, school, etc., don't make promises just to break them, and don't say things just because you feel like it. Become

CHAPTER FIVE: ACCEPT RESPONSIBILITY

someone who is trustworthy and dependable in what is required of you.

Sometimes people have the best intentions but do not yield positive impact because of their lack of execution. In such instances, it is mere talk that leads to nowhere.

Don't just talk about all the things that you are going to do, deliver on them! Be a person that's known for your ability to deliver on your word. If you say something is going to be done, do it!

Our thoughts and words alone don't always lead to progress, but it's the application of our thoughts and words put into action that makes the big difference!

Learn to Say No

To live your best life, you will have to constantly identify the things that you must say No to. Of course, we all know there are certain toxic relationships and environments that we can easily identify and make the decision to say No to. However, there can also be some good-intentioned advice that we should politely refuse because it will derail us from achieving our goals.

For example, if your friend suggests you go out when you know you've already set a budget, you must be able to say No and avoid going over your budget. Shopping may be one of the few ways you de-stress. However, when you know that it will put you over your budget, you should say No to the urge to go shopping.

Get outside of your comfort zones: Be willing to get outside of your comfort zone because Living Your Best Life will require doing things outside of what you are accustomed to doing. You must get outside of your current routine, habits, and cycle. Be willing to do things that you may not want to do but need to do. Growth is never convenient, and it doesn't just happen. This is why you must be prepared to move outside of what's comfortable.

To be what you've never been, you must be willing to do what you've never done.

Sometimes, you've got to get out of your circle to make your biggest impact. In some of those moments, you'll actually be rejected by those closest to you as they can be your biggest doubters or haters. Luke 4:24 shows us that Jesus Himself was not accepted in His hometown because people obviously doubted His ability.

Mark adds, *"Then Jesus told them, a prophet is honored everywhere except in his own hometown and among his relatives and his own family"* Mark 6:4. Matthew 13:57 continues, *"And they were deeply offended and refused to believe in him. Then Jesus told them: 'A prophet is honored everywhere except in his own hometown and among his family.'"*

You can see from these verses that people who are closest to you may doubt your ability. They may look at your past, or the mistakes of your parents and may doubt you, and hold certain things against you, and then limit you to only what they can believe of you. They may believe that your past will always determine your present, as well as your future. But that doesn't have to be true. Your past does not have to be your present, nor does it have to be your future.

All the more reason why, you have to be willing to always believe in yourself, and believe what God says about you ad be willing to get outside of your comfort zone and those things that that are most familiar, and stretch yourself.

Supernatural things happen when you get out of your comfort zone. The supernatural things only happen when you take risks. The supernatural doesn't happen inside of your comfort zone.

You can make the impossible possible by trusting in God and getting out of your comfort zone and taking a risk.

Think about it. You can't create something new by simply doing what everybody else is doing. You can't create something new by just staying in your comfort zone. You have to be willing to jump outside of it and take risks.

Don't just read the credits of the stories of other people's lives. Take action and create stories in your own life! Don't just read about the heroes of the world and in the Bible. Do things in your own life to make great things happen!

Be Set Apart

We were all uniquely created with different gifts. Embrace your uniqueness and set yourself apart. Don't set your goal to be normal or average or to be like everyone else because you weren't created to be just like everyone else. You were created to be you.

Become comfortable with the fact that you can't please everyone and that it isn't your life mission or goal to do so. Rather, live your life to please God and worry less about what others have to say; prioritize what God has to say over what others may have to say.

Those that live their best life walk in purpose and are very deliberate in every action they take. You have to embrace being different and not always looking to fit in or conform to others' standards.

In being set apart, you must value your time and spend it purposefully. Before you commit to every time-consuming activity, ask yourself if it is the best use of your time. Is there something valuable to be gained from the activity?

You can't just wander through each day without a sense of purpose. You must spend your time wisely and move differently.

Walk with purpose in your step!

It seems to be all about being politically correct nowadays. In order to live your best life, you've got to be willing to go against the grain at times because what is politically correct may not always be spiritually correct. When that is the case, you've got to have the courage to stand up and do what may not be politically correct. You can't always just conform to what everyone else is doing or saying. Sometimes you've got to take a stand for what is spiritually correct over what is politically correct.

Don't be too "politically correct."

A few years ago, Chick-Fil-A took a stand for what it believed in. The company chose its spiritual values over being politically correct. It took a stance on a certain topic it believed was spiritually correct according to scripture and didn't shy away from standing firm on its beliefs, even though it might have been politically correct to take another stance or put out something to retract their initial viewpoint. For the things that you believe in, you must be willing to take a stance.

Chick-Fil-A also has made it a point to close its restaurant operations on Sundays based upon their religious beliefs. Even though its competition is open on Sundays, Chick-Fil-A continues to capture great market share over its competitors, despite being open for business one less day than their competitors, while standing firm to the principles that the company believes in as well as daring to be set apart.

CHAPTER FIVE: ACCEPT RESPONSIBILITY

To live your best life, you can't be afraid to be set apart.

Exercise

- List the things that are consuming your time but aren't helping you walk further in your purpose.

Chapter Six

Be Innovative

Don't do life simply out of tradition, or simply out of memory, or simply out of the things that you see in your present. **Do life out of imagination!**

Living Your Best Life often requires you to be innovative. It means being willing to try and learn new things. It means putting your innate creative nature to use. It means not always just being stuck in old ways and old habits and old traditions. Being innovative involves being able to think and see outside of your present situation. Being innovative entails taking the steps to learn a new craft or study new information and make necessary changes.

Being innovative means being proactive rather than just reactive. Not simply just always reacting to what happens, but also doing things to allow oneself to be better prepared in advance. Being an innovator means bringing something new to the table. Being an innovator is a person that brings about change. Being an innovator helps create new things.

There are so many things that we see every day all around us, on our jobs, in our communities, in our schools, in our world that need to be fixed or need to be enhanced. There are so many problems that we all see and we all can easily name. We usually talk quite often about all the things that are wrong. But we must also begin to realize that every problem presents an equal opportunity to be solved. We need to be innovators and help create and bring about that change. We are here to innovate. We are here to make new things happen. Innovation doesn't just apply to technology, it applies to how we go about doing things in our lives.

An innovator is needed to help bring about the change that you see is needed in your community. An innovator is needed to create better ways to connect with our children that seem to be lost. An innovator is needed to create that business that's going to meet those needs and solve the problems, issues and inconveniences that you see.

Be an innovator, find ways to make things better! The world is waiting on you!

Become the Reader

Become a reader because leaders are readers. The most successful people in the world are all readers because in doing so, they constantly expose themselves to information and knowledge that help them become better. It doesn't matter if you prefer print books, e-books, or audiobooks, you've got to read and learn new things.

How can you constantly be learning new things, if you don't read?

If you want to become more knowledgeable about something, find a way to read more about it. Reading exposes you to so much more information and helps broaden and enhance your perspectives on things. Great wisdom is gained through reading. Think about it for a second, we learn more about God and His Word through the act of Reading His Word. To know what God has said about something for ourselves, we must Read His Word. To know more about the principles and promises, we Read His Word.

CHAPTER SIX: BE INNOVATIVE

So just as we are to read and study the Word to gain the greatest wisdom from God, we should also look to read to gain wisdom on topics and areas that help us to grow here on Earth in our professional endeavors. It is important that we apply the discipline of reading to our routine habits. One of the best ways to elevate your mind is to read!

Write Things Down

There are so many benefits in writing important things down. If you are anywhere where you can learn something, always bring a notebook to write things down because by writing things down it serves as a point of record. It helps you to capture the valuable and important information so that you can later reference it and refer to it, to help you along your way. No matter how good a message is, or how good a conference is, or how much valuable information has been presented, if you do not write it down, you will forget so many valuable points.

Many times, we hear a prophetic message and it resonates within us and we feel good about it, but if we don't write things down and take notes, not even a week later, if we want to revert to our take away points and things that we want to apply to our lives, we have already forgotten. I encourage you to make it a habit to write things down and to always keep a notebook. I recommend writing down things related to your craft or profession, such as meeting notes, training notes, daily/weekly tasks and responsibilities, plans, goals, as well as recording your life lessons and reflections.

I also recommend having multiple notebooks, one notebook that you dedicate for your professional notes and resources and another for your personal development and resources. This is a small but helpful tool because you can always go back and reference all your notes related to your personal development in one central place and any professional related notes can be retrieved from another central location. Also, be sure that you include dates when you write things down.

By writing things down, including your goals, you become ten times more likely to follow through and achieve those things that are written down as opposed to just keeping them in your mind.

What Are You Speaking?

> *Death and life are in the power of the tongue, and those who love it will eat its fruits.* -**Proverbs 18:21**

In order to live your best life, you must declare and affirm good things. You must speak life. You must speak truth! To know this truth, you will have to meditate on scriptures and find positive words of affirmation. Pay attention to what comes out of your mouth because life and death are in the power of your tongue (Proverbs 18:21). You must know that what you say about something can have such a huge impact. What you begin to say to yourself and what you begin to speak, you affirm and that usually becomes your reality.

Be very careful about the words that come out of your mouth. Be careful about what it is that you are telling yourself, as well as others. You can't constantly be saying to yourself that I am a failure or always telling yourself that you are not good enough, or not smart enough, or that you can't do something. If you keep speaking these things, you are reaffirming to yourself and putting it out there that you can't.

You must speak words of life! Be an optimist, not a pessimist. Look to find the good in yourself. Look to find the good in the situation and speak on the opportunities as your primary point of focus as opposed to dwelling and speaking on the negatives only. While sometimes you must speak the hard truths and deal with reality in order to make

CHAPTER SIX: BE INNOVATIVE

progress, you should always seek to speak about even the hard truths in the most positive manner.

- What you declare over your life matters
- What you declare over your year matters
- Your words call into existence what is not yet seen!
- It's important to declare good things! What are you declaring?
- The way that you see you and God sees you is totally different!
- God created you as an excellent masterpiece! God created you to be GREAT!
- Start seeing yourself as God does.
- Life and death are in the power of the tongue.
- Our words can give life or they can kill.
- The words that you speak over yourself and over the situation are prophetic
- Declarations frame your future
- Declarations call into existence the things that do not yet exists

"I tell you the truth, you can say to this mountain, 'May you be lifted up and thrown into the sea,' and it will happen. But you must really believe it will happen and have no doubt in your heart." Mark 11:23.

"And a small rudder makes a huge ship turn wherever the pilot chooses to go, even though the winds are strong. In the same way, the tongue is a small thing that makes grand speeches. But a tiny spark can set a great forest on fire. James 3:4-5

- We are driven in the direction of our words.
- Declarations will determine your deliverance.
- If you are going through the valley, God is going to get you through
- Your valley is not your finale!

Chapter Seven

Self-Discipline

Self-discipline is one of the most essential keys to achieving success and reaping the rewards of your best life. Discipline is what you must have in order to combat your excuses.

Brian Tracy says it best: "You can achieve almost any goal you set for yourself if you have the discipline to pay the price, to do what you need to do, and to never give up."

Many times, it's not that we don't know WHAT to do, but rather we don't have the DISCIPLINE to make ourselves do what needs to be done.

> *Your ability to think, plan and work hard in the short-term and to discipline yourself to do what is right and necessary before you do what is fun and easy is the key to creating a wonderful future for yourself.* **-Brian Tracy**

To live your life to the fullest, you must have self-discipline. Discipline means the ability to say No to certain things.

Discipline in Exercise

Have a goal to live as long as you possibly can. This includes having discipline in your health habits. As you increase your energy, there is a resulting increase in your overall happiness. Energy is also linked to educational attainment, creativity, and assertiveness. The more energy you have, the more creative you're likely to be and the more likely you'll speak up for yourself and take action towards your dreams.

Exercise can increase the production of endorphins, which are known to help produce positive feelings and reduce the perception of pain. It increases your energy levels and helps control your weight. It helps prevent excess weight gain and maintain weight loss.

Exercise sharpens your wits. Physical activity boosts blood flow to the brain, which may help maintain brain function. It also promotes good lung function, a characteristic of people whose memories and mental acuity remain strong as they age. While all types of physical activity help keep your mind sharp, many studies have shown that aerobic exercise in particular successfully improves cognitive function.

Eat Right. Be mindful of what you eat and what you put into your body. Do your research and study what's best for you and your health! Make it a priority to prioritize your physical health.

Exercise

- Write a daily or weekly exercise plan.
- Begin exercising if you aren't already doing so.

CHAPTER SEVEN: SELF-DISCIPLINE

Three Declarations to Make Every Day

1. Declare freedom over your past

Get over your past. Don't let your past become your prison. Your past does not define you. You become new in Christ and become a new creature.

Your past is a point of reference not your residence.

You have to declare freedom over pain and offense over your past.

As long as you keep holding on to the past, it keeps your burdened and holds you back.

2. Declare peace over your problems

Everybody has problems. Jesus says you are going to have problems but have cheer I have overcome this world.

You need to say Peace Be still over your storms.

Jesus said even you will do even greater works than he, if you believe!

Sometimes you need to stop telling God always about how big your problems are but tell your problems how big your God is.

3. Declare hope over your future

Declare that your best is yet to come!

Don't let your outward conditions affect the conditions of your heart in a negative way.

Think about what comes out of your mouth much of the time. Do you always complain and grumble about things? Do you use your voice and speak life into your situation? Do you use your voice to speak life into others and their situations? Does what come out of your mouth, building something or someone up? Or is it usually tearing someone or something down?

Life and death are in the power of the tongue. Choose to speak life over your situation. Choose to speak positive things. Choose to expose yourself to positivity.

Exercise

- Research the scriptures to identify a verse or passage relating to what you're believing God to do for you in your life and write it down
- Meditate and recite the words of truth every day.
- Pray on them.
- Find motivational quotes and meditate on them to stay inspired

If you are believing God to give you wisdom, search scriptures on wisdom. If you are believing God for healing, find scriptures on healing. You may use Google for assistance or popular websites such as www.openbible.info to provide many scriptures that focus on what you're believing for.

Support Yourself

To live your best life, you've got to be able to encourage and support yourself, even when others around you don't always encourage or support you, including loved ones, friends and colleagues, as there will be times when you may not receive any support.

You must realize that it is not ultimately anyone else's job to support you. While of course, we all want support and seek to put ourselves in environments where we do have & can gain support, but the hard truth is that it's YOUR job to support YOU! Other people's support, or lack of support, should not determine whether YOU pursue your

CHAPTER SEVEN: SELF-DISCIPLINE

passions, walk in your purpose, and make the determination to live your best life.

Your life was ultimately created for you! So long as you maintain the right mindset and the belief in what has been placed within your heart, and continue to drive towards fulfilling those desires, that is all you need. You must also realize that the more success you have and the more impact and influence you have, the more you will gain supporters and believers. The downside is you will also gain more "haters" and doubters.

You must determine in your mind that you are not going to let other people's opinions deter you from your destiny or from Living Your Best Life! Because someone will always have something to say. And you cannot please everybody. In living our best life, we must get to the point where naysayers, negativity, critics, and doubters don't adversely affect us and we become mature enough to use it as fuel to simply become better and exercise even greater resilience.

You can't let everything get the best of you and your emotions. Get to the point where you no longer allow certain things to steal your mood. You just let it roll off, like water off a duck's back.

Ignore the Haters

In order to live your best life, you have to be able to ignore the doubters, the haters, the critics and the naysayers. Understand that anytime you begin taking action and making things happen, there will always be someone that will have something negative to say. It is inevitable. You cannot be a person of impact and 100% liked by EVERYONE! It is just not going to happen. So don't even worry about trying to make that your goal.

It is not your goal to please and appease everyone.

Your goal is to maximize your potential, walk in your purpose, be an example, impact others for the better and live your best life! Your goal is to control YOU and the things that you do. The actions that you take, the things that you can control! Your focus is to focus on doing the things that it takes to live your best. Focus on how you can become a better servant, how you can become a better Christian, how you can become a better parent, focus on how you can encourage and inspire others, focus on how you can improve your business, focus on how you can become better at your craft, focus on how you can become more patient, focus on how you can become more disciplined, focus on how you can become more productive, focus on the things that you can control that enable you to live your best life.

And as you do that and allow that to be your point of focus, nothing else really matters. As long as you are putting forth your best effort and constantly improving, NO ONE else's negative opinions, criticism and doubt really matters.

If you are walking here on this Earth, know that you will have haters, doubters, and critics.

Even the most perfect person to ever walk the Earth, Jesus Christ, had plenty of haters, doubters and critics and he was perfect. So you should automatically know that you too would have haters. But haters, doubters and critics have no power to stop you from Living Your Best Life and being impactful. Yes, they may even try different tactics to try and derail you, but in the end, you cannot keep a good man/woman down.

What you sow is what you reap. And our God sees all. So don't get caught up in the hating, the criticism, the doubters and various tactics that may even be tried, just know that in the end what you sow you will reap, and only you can stop you. Only you can stop you, by listening

CHAPTER SEVEN: SELF-DISCIPLINE

to that negativity and buying into it yourself. Haters, doubters and critics, cannot stop you! Their opinion does not have to be your reality!

Expect there to be haters anytime there is progress that is being made. As often times the haters are only jealous, for whatever reasons. And if you don't have any haters or doubters, perhaps maybe you need to check your pulse and see if you are still living and/or if you're actually making any progress. Progress is going to be met with rejection and/or resistance.

To Whom Much Is Given, Much Is Required

It's important to know that to whom much is given, much is required (Luke 12:48). This means you must delve deep into God's word to discover your gifts and then begin to use them to fulfill the commandment of fruitfulness that God gave in Genesis 1 after He created man. The more you continue to utilize the gifts that God gave, the more you're blessed with next-level opportunities. And know that those opportunities come with greater responsibilities.

Sometimes we want to be promoted to the next level, yet we are not always ready for that next level of responsibility. For example, if I want to be a CEO of a company but lack sound principles on how to spend or manage money, or how to effectively work with others, and how to run a business, then I may not be able to handle the responsibilities that come with the position at the current moment. If you're currently so overwhelmed in your current position that may include just managing yourself at this point in time, how do you expect to be ready to manage twenty to fifty other lives? That would be more of a burden than a blessing if that did happen at that current moment.

To become ready, you must begin to master your current level and areas of responsibility.

Take Pride in What You Do

> *Whatever you do, work heartily, as for the Lord and not for men, knowing that from the Lord you will receive the inheritance as your reward. You are serving the Lord Christ.*
> **-Colossians 3:23-24**

It's important to understand that whatever environment or current job you may be placed in, whether it's ideal or not, you must take pride in it. Remember that whatever we do, we are a representative of not only the company in which we may work for but also our personal brand/reputation, and even most importantly, a representative on behalf of the kingdom of God.

So, the way that we work should be done in excellence, as we are working unto the Lord. We should be willing to give our best to God, and we should earn a reputation as diligent people who execute and get the job done. God is the connection to your breakthrough. You must put in the work, and it starts wherever you are, and if you do so, he'll be sure to reward you and open doors, beyond your imagination. But you can't give half "behind" effort and expect to receive breakthrough and next level success. It starts with taking pride in what you do, right where you are.

How you handle your current situation is a pre-cursor to your future situation. Don't wait until you "arrive" at your most ideal job or situation before you begin to take pride in what you do, because honestly, if you wait for that, you will be waiting your entire lifetime. It all starts right where you are. Place a quality value on where you currently are and what you're currently doing so you can take advantage of next-level opportunities. Stop grumbling and start being productive right where you are. And remember to be proud of the little steps of progress that

CHAPTER SEVEN: SELF-DISCIPLINE

you make along the way. You must value every opportunity and put forth your best efforts wherever you are.

2 Corinthians 9:6 says, *"The point is this, whoever sows sparingly will also reap sparingly, and whoever sows bountifully will also reap bountifully."* Galatians 6:7 also says, *"Do not be deceived. God is not mocked, for whatever one sows, he will reap."*

Remember that taking pride or being faithful one day or one month, or six months, doesn't necessarily mean your opportunity will come immediately. Know that as you remain faithful and diligent, you're planting seeds. In due time, you'll reap your harvest from those seeds.

Living Your Best Life is manifested when you can overcome the tendency to cut corners or look for easy ways out. Be willing to do more than what you're paid to do. Go above and beyond and do more than the minimum requirements.

Most people are only willing to do the bare minimum just to get by. Many maintain the status quo and never look to elevate their standard of living. What do your habits look like? What is your work ethic like?

Be Able to be Trusted

Make sure you master where you are and are able to be trusted right where you currently are. In order to continue to grow in responsibility and grow in opportunity, you first have to master what's in front of you and be able to be trusted with what you have.

Meaning that if you want to become the boss, CEO or want to make next level type money or whatever it may be, you have to first be able to handle what you have. If you can't handle or respect following the rules of working for someone else, then you can't expect to become a boss and everyone just automatically follow your rules. If you can't handle or manage money know, but want greater financial responsibility, that will actual only lead to greater financial burden. Because if you don't yet have the discipline to master your current situation, being promoted will only lead to bigger issues. If you want a new car and you don't take care of your current one, and don't make sure you keep it up, then having a more expensive car will only lead to greater issues because it soon will have maintenance issues.

Stay Hungry

> *Take pride in what you do and let the quality of your work be your signature.* **-Kloby**

You should be content but not complacent. There is a difference between the two. Being complacent means being so satisfied with your own abilities or situation that you feel you don't need to try any harder. You should avoid this by constantly striving to be the best you can be. Never get to the point where you are so complacent with yourself or your situation, that you stop seeking to learn, that you stop seeking to grow, that you stop seeking to innovate, that you stop being adaptable. If you do, that is when you will begin to decline, and you'll no longer be walking in your best life.

Being content means that you are grateful and appreciative of things. It's about having a sense of appreciation for wherever you may be in life. There are things to be grateful for even if your current situation is not exactly what you want. You can always find good in your current situation. So be content, while also staying hungry and driven to be the best you can be!

Stay driven to accomplish all the things that you can achieve!

Stay driven in your pursuit of continuously improving and making progress! You've got to stay hungry for more, more of the greatness that God has in store for you! You've got to stay hungry in your pursuit

CHAPTER SEVEN: SELF-DISCIPLINE

of being your best self! Nothing is going to just come, nothing is going to just happen by chance. You've got to be driven to be the best, to be your best! Don't be complacent!

Push yourself to elevate your standard of living. Set the bar of excellence in your life. Living Your Best Life entails helping to raise and set the standard.

Chapter Eight

Financial Excellence

We should always strive to be financially independent and leave an inheritance for our loved ones. Proverbs 13:22 says, *"A good person leaves an inheritance for their children's children, but a sinner's wealth is stored up for the righteous"* (NIV).

The primary reason for financial problems in life is a lack of self-discipline. In clear-cut language, the inability to delay gratification in the short term causes financial issues. We tend to spend all that we earn or borrow more often than we should.

Statistics show that the average American family has a net worth of only about $8,000.

However, the good news is that we are living in one of the best times to be able to achieve financial independence, wealth and prosperity, as there are more pipelines than ever to generate income and to also help you save. In Living Your Best Life, you must become excited about saving your money and not just spending it. You become excited about how much you have set aside or saved for a rainy day or for an inheritance to help bless your children or others.

As you save, remember to give God His portion first through tithing. Give him the first ten percent out of every dollar you earn. Then, pay yourself second. This means you should set aside some money for savings. Advisers say you need to save twenty percent of what you earn to be financially independent for life.

Think about this for a second. While there's nothing wrong with buying things for yourself, you need to go about it the right way. If you spend all your money on clothes, shoes, credit card payments, and all other things without saving, you're simply working just to pay someone else. You're not looking out for yourself. If you spend all your money without saving some, think about what will happen in the case of an emergency.

As you tithe and set aside money for future use, make sure you create yourself a budget and tailor your living needs around your budget. Within your budget, you should allocate the amount to set aside for tithing, for savings, the amount set for any other giving/charitable donations, the amount set for food and grocery, the amount set for mortgage/rent, vehicle payments, any applicable insurance payments, and an amount set for any special projects or vacation trips.

Living Your Best Life is not striving to simply get by living from paycheck to paycheck. Living Your Best Life means being financially independent. However, I must also put this disclaimer out there. Whatever your current financial status, never associate your self-worth with the amount of money in your bank account. Finances are temporary. Only the things that we do for Christ will last eternally.

I advocate that we should seek to be the very best we can be in every aspect of our lives. This includes being financially independent and not indebted to others. I also strongly believe that our God is a

CHAPTER EIGHT: FINANCIAL EXCELLENCE

supplier, a provider who wants us to be prosperous so that we can be a blessing to others.

Understand that, as you grow financially, it becomes your responsibility to also bless others. God blesses us so that we can help others and bring greater glory to His name.

Remember

- Tithe and give God your first 10 percent
- Set a budget
- Pay yourself and save 20 percent
- Live off the remaining 70 percent

Note that the savings are post-tax. They are calculated using what you receive once taxes have been paid. If you need help calculating the percentage that needs to be saved, tithed, and spent, here is an example:

If my income is $750 dollars and I want to know what 5 percent is, I would put this in my calculator: $750 x .05 = $37.5

If I want to know what 11 percent is, I would put this in my calculator: $750 x .11 = $82.5

The 1 Percent Formula

This formula will help you save twenty percent of your income (after paying your tithe and taxes). When using the formula for saving, start with a number you're comfortable with. It can be as little as one percent. Then, increase your percentage of savings by one percent each month until you arrive at the point where you can comfortably save twenty percent of all the income you earn.

Exercise

Create or establish a Financial Freedom account that is separate from all your other accounts. It should also be an account that isn't easily tied to the rest of your accounts.

Ideally, you want to be able to put money into this account easily, but not be able to pull or draw from it as easily or without penalty. Some savings accounts have a limit on the number of withdrawals or transfers you can make in a given time. Even though I am not necessarily advocating any specific type of account at this time for your financial freedom account, I am just recommending that you create one.

You can use Google to search for different applications that help you automatically save money each month. There are many different applications out there that can help in this regard. Use the one percent formula.

Spend Money on Assets

In Living Your Best Life, you want to use wisdom in how you spend your money. Make sure that you are spending most of your money on things that are assets. An asset is a resource with economic value that an individual, corporation, or country owns or controls with the expectation that it will provide a future benefit, while liabilities are your obligations that must be paid or services that must be performed. It really all comes down to this: think about your most recent purchases. Have you been spending more money on liabilities or assets? For most people, dollars spent on liabilities far outweigh the amount spent on assets.

CHAPTER EIGHT: FINANCIAL EXCELLENCE

The critical difference in the basic spending habits of financially successful and wealthy people is that they spend the majority of their money on acquiring assets.

Some common examples of assets are:

- Stock market
- Real estate (rental homes, condos, strip malls, storage units to rent out)
- Ventures that generate semi-passive income (website, blog, YouTube, Instagram, affiliate marketing)

Some examples of liabilities are:

- Cell phones
- TVs
- Credit card debt
- Student loans
- Automobile loans
- Boat loans

Most times we spend money on things that yield us no return. Assets are things that are going to give value back to us.

Chapter Nine

True Goals of Life

For I know the plans I have for you, declares the Lord, plans to prosper you and not to harm you, plans to give you hope and a future. -**Jeremiah 29:11**

When things happen, we have two options: retreat and do absolutely nothing, which is another form of retreating or use the situation to drive you to become better.

The decision is up to you!

You will have things happen to you in life. You won't be problem free. You won't have this fairy tale life where nothing ever goes wrong. That is not the case! But in Living Your Best Life you have the right mindset and can take the right course of action to not allow things to defeat you, and you commit to being better as a result of whatever happens.

Whatever happens, determine to find a way to use it to become even better. Even in the midst of success and growth, still look to continuously improve. If you have defeats, illness, death, or adverse circumstances that happen to you, use it to become even better. That's Living Your Best Life!

You can do ANYTHING

In Living Your Best Life, you know that you can do and accomplish anything you put your mind to. Paul tells us that we "*can do everything through Christ who gives [us] strength*" (Philippians 4:13. And again, *"I can do all things through Christ who strengthens me."* Philippians 4:13.

We must see how powerful this verse is. The scripture reveals that we can do ALL THINGS through Christ who strengthens us, who empowers us, who enables us to accomplish whatever we set our minds to do.

Notice how this scripture also references the responsibility given to you. The responsibility is on you. We know that God is all-powerful, all knowing, and all-present, but He enables us to have the responsibility to achieve greatness—to achieve whatever we set our minds to do. This scripture is not just talking about the power of God as the focal point but is referring to us as the initiator and focal point. We already know that God can do all things! And in this scripture, Paul reminds us about the power that we have through Christ. This scripture is about You! It clearly reveals what you can do!

God gives us the power of choice. He gives us all the power to make our own decisions. In essence, it's not up to God to determine how blessed, impactful, or successful you are. It depends upon you.

God has great plans in store for each of us, more than we could ever think or imagine for ourselves. So, whether you walk in those blessings that He has, whether you receive all the great things He has for you, it is ultimately dependent upon you. It starts with You!

It starts with us, and then we let Him use us, strengthen us, and direct us—so that we can receive and accomplish the great things that He has for us.

CHAPTER NINE: TRUE GOALS OF LIFE

The question is will you make the decision to believe that you can do anything through Christ who strengthens you? If you don't believe it, then you are not only limiting yourself but also limiting your perception of God and His power and ability.

You must understand that you play a huge part in determining your own success. And you must first believe it. As you do, and begin to take action, listen and allow Christ to strengthen you in the things you do—then anything can be possible! Anything can be accomplished by you through Him!

Think about all the great things here on earth—all the great inventions, all the great architecture, all the great artists and designs. Airplanes, cars, electricity, light bulb, computers, the Internet, electricity, boats, tools, batteries, antibiotics, cures, x-ray machines, televisions, camera, telephones, different genres and types of music, film, printing press, the Eiffel Tower, Taj Mahal, the Great Pyramid, Mount Rushmore, the Roman Colosseum, the Great Wall of China, hospitals, and foundations that help those that are in need were created and invented by people just like you and me. You just must believe you can do anything and know that, if you put in the work necessary and allow God to provide you with the strength, wisdom, and direction, you can achieve anything!

Many times, the only major differences between those that do great things and those who don't come down to three factors:

The belief system. Those that achieve great things believe it's possible! Even if/when the majority doesn't think it's possible or can be done, they believe it can be achieved!

Work ethic. Based upon the belief system that it is possible, the great achievers are willing to put in the work necessary. They are willing to make the necessary sacrifices, to put in the time and investment, to study and learn what needs to be learned, and to move outside their comfort zones when most others aren't willing to do these things to the degree that is necessary.

If you have an average work ethic and average work habits, you can't live your best life. You can't be all you were created to be. You can't accomplish all that is in store for you by having average work habits.

Relentless faith. They believe that it's all going to work out in the end. They believe that what they sow, they will reap. They believe that, in the end, it's going to work out. So, they don't ever give up. They too have all had doubts, fears, questions, times of disbelief. They have all reached a breaking point at some time or another and wanted to quit, to throw in the towel. Somehow, however, they all made it a point to keep going, and they never gave up! Never give up.

> *When you are resilient and relentless, the quitter in you can't quit because the winner in you won't allow the quitter to quit or give up regardless of the Who or the Why.-* **Dharius Daniels**

Life Principles

> *Hold yourself responsible for a higher standard than anyone else expects of you. Never excuse yourself. Never pity yourself. Be a hard master to yourself and be lenient to everyone else.* - **Henry Ward Beecher**

Don't settle

I want you to know something vital now: do not ever settle for anything less than your best and less than your worth. I know that can be difficult sometimes, but it is essential that you keep chasing

CHAPTER NINE: TRUE GOALS OF LIFE

after your very best life. The emphasis here is on chasing. Perfection cannot be attained—at least on earth—but we can keep striving. Someone who tries will ultimately become better than the person who is content with remaining in the same spot.

Don't obsess over attention

In today's world, with the dominance of social media and other media outlets, so many people obsess over attention. They obsess over their posts going viral, how many likes they can get, or how many people view them. This can possibly lead to great distraction. Many times, we can get distracted by being so caught up in seeking attention, making sure that everyone sees you and sees your post or video, and gaining attention that we miss the actual experience.

To live your best life, be in the moment and enjoy the experiences without always being distracted by social media. Don't be obsessive over seeking attention, especially that is not benefitting or building anyone else up. Don't value yourself based upon the amount of attention that you get on social media or by the number of likes that you get.

Don't be Jealous

It is simple: don't allow jealousy to consume you if you wish to live a highly fulfilling life. Rather, the focus should be on being the best you. Jealousy takes away time and energy by deterring you from concentrating on the things that are most important in your own life.

I want you to be happy for others.

Be willing to see them shine and live their best lives. Even if it seems they are not working as hard as you, remain happy for them and celebrate their accomplishments.

Know that the beautiful things God has for you cannot be taken away from you. Sometimes it may be hard to see others being blessed while you continue to remain in your current season or predicament. Still, don't allow jealousy to take over.

Also, don't look to find fault with other people and then begin to justify your reasons why you think they shouldn't be successful. Swallow your pride and draw lessons or seek help from others on how you can also succeed!

Asking for advice is not looking for a handout.

Don't be afraid to fail

Fear is one of the greatest factors that hinder progress and personal development. The fear of failure and the fear of success are two of the most prevalent fears experienced by people generally. To live your best life, you must embrace fear and declare that your faith will be greater than your fear!

Don't run away from fear; confront it. In reality, the things that we are most fearful of are never actually as bad as we think. I believe the message is don't be afraid to fail because all successful people have failed at some point. The scariest thing to do is to live a life filled with "what ifs" and die empty.

There are too many people in this world who die with unfulfilled potential and unrealized dreams because they were afraid to fail.

You must define failure as an event and not a person. This means that failing at something doesn't make you a failure. It's simply an event—it doesn't define you. Also, understand that failure can also be a precursor to success. If we reflect and have a growth mindset, we can learn valuable information from our failures, which will make us better and better equipped for success.

CHAPTER NINE: TRUE GOALS OF LIFE

You must decide which is greater: your faith or your fear. At every turn, your faith should be greater than your fear!

Most successful people point to various hard times in their lives that helped propel them towards their success. Here are some of those people:

- Bill Gates' first attempt at developing his unique Windows application failed. However, he viewed the failure as an impetus, and it helped him to become the richest man in the world for many years.
- Tyler Perry was once homeless but now has his own production company and is worth more than $100 million.
- Oprah Winfrey was repeatedly molested by her cousin, uncle, and a family friend. She became pregnant at 14 and ran away from home before eventually becoming the world's first female billionaire.
- Jay-Z couldn't land a record deal in his earlier days. Now he has one of the most successful record labels, as well as other successful businesses.
- Michael Jordan was cut from the varsity team of his high school basketball team but went on to become the greatest player of all time.
- Walt Disney, the man behind the "happiest place on earth," was fired by the editor of a newspaper because he "lacked imagination and had no good ideas." He then started several businesses that failed and ended in bankruptcy. Nonetheless, that didn't stop him from bringing life to one of the most beloved animated characters, Mickey Mouse, and becoming the recipient of 22 Academy Awards.
- Abraham Lincoln once said, "My great concern is not whether you have failed, but whether you are content with your failure." He had his share of failure and defeat before

becoming one of our nation's greatest leaders. Thirty years prior to winning the presidential election, he lost his job, failed at business, had a nervous breakdown, and lost eight elections. Instead of giving into the failure, he persisted to become the 16th President of the United States of America.

- Steve Jobs dropped out of college and quit his first job to "find himself." This didn't stop the Apple mastermind from becoming wildly successful. Even along the path to success, he was unceremoniously forced to leave the company that he started. Upon his return years later, he brought with him innovation and a drive that made Apple the world's most iconic and successful technology brands.
- Shaqueem Griffin, who lost his hand at a very young age, overcame his adversity and made it to the NFL. Officially, it is on record that he has the fastest 40-yard dash by a person at his position.
- Neale Donald Walsh once said that life begins at the end of your comfort zone. When you feel the pain of bad experiences, creativity will allow you to turn that experience into gain. When going through different seasons and experiences, instead of being discouraged and angry, let these experiences stir your creative spirit.

Don't be afraid to fail. Try new things, test out new things! Go after what you believe in!

We all will fail! It's just really all about how we respond to failure. Because even all of the great figures that we look up to have All failed! But the difference is in how we respond to failure. The successful use failure as an opportunity to learn from to become even better. They don't let failure keep them from continuing to move forward. Even in failure, you can learn so many valuable lessons. So don't be afraid to go after whatever has been placed in your heart and whatever you believe in. Don't let your fear be greater than your faith! If you believe in something, put in the proper planning and research, and go after it!

Have Faith over Fear! Remember you can do All things, through the One who strengthens you.

So, only you and your own measure of faith can be the only things that can stop you. If you don't have much faith and don't believe in yourself and don't believe in the God you serve, then failure maybe likely, but that's because of your own perception! And you can change that!

Big goals, big dreams, big visions, all require BIG faith!

So instead of building up your fear, or dwelling on how and why you can't succeed, spend that energy building up your faith and your belief in what is possible and who you have on your side!

Leave a Legacy

According to the Webster's dictionary, legacy can succinctly be described as "Anything handed down from the past, as from an ancestor or predecessor." This shows a good legacy is a very important thing that we should be looking to hand down because it is never irrelevant. Your legacy is determined by what you have done in terms of your contribution to knowledge, innovations, and helping others. If you are not doing these things on a regular basis, you are not leaving a good legacy.

I want you to remember that what you did at the end of your life is not what shapes your legacy. Rather, it is what you are presently doing that counts. How are you rectifying your past mistakes? When you adopt the right leadership skills, you will ultimately leave a great legacy, but these leadership skills can only be adopted when you have the right attitude.

Be a leader and leave a legacy.

Leaders lead by example. You don't ask others to do things that you aren't willing to do yourself.

Be Great

> *The measure of a man is in the lives he's touched.* **-Ernie Banks**

You can't be great without influencing others, because greatness requires you to impact something beyond just yourself. It is imperative that we strive to be great because that's what we were created to be! You were created to make a mark, an impact on this world! It's up to you whether you walk in that greatness.

We must strive daily to ponder the kind of legacies we can leave behind. Would you be rather known as the guy who just "tried" or the one who pushed through when things were difficult and challenging?

American entrepreneur, Jim Rohn said, "All good men and women must take responsibility to create legacies that will take the next generation to a level we could only imagine." Inspirational author Shannon L. Alder put it better when she said, "Carve your name on hearts, not tombstones. A legacy is etched into the minds of others and the stories they share about you."

Exercise

- Define your legacy.

Understanding the Seasons

> *For everything there is a season, a time for every activity under heaven. A time to be born and a time to die. A time to plant and a time to harvest. A time to kill and a time to heal. A*

> *time to tear down and a time to build up. A time to cry and a time to laugh. A time to grieve and a time to dance. A time to scatter stones and a time to gather stones. A time to embrace and a time to turn away. A time to search and a time to quit searching. A time to keep and a time to throw away. A time to tear and a time to mend. A time to be quiet and a time to speak. A time to love and a time to hate. A time for war and a time for peace.* **-Eccleiastes 3: 1-8**

I want you to know that there will be different seasons in your life. Everything in life is seasonal and, whatever season you may be in, know that it serves a purpose. During crisis, remember that seasons are temporary. In seasons of abundance, continue to remain focused on the plan for your future. Winter never stays forever; neither does summer.

Remember that nothing is permanent but God and His word. This is why, no matter the season, you should seek to learn the valuable lessons that He is teaching in your current season. Nothing just happens. There is always a lesson or opportunity in it all.

God created the seasons with a specific purpose, and this makes all of them important.

Spring is a time of beginnings: new life, possibilities, and potential. There is a feeling of vibrancy and energy. It is when the farmer plants seeds.

Summer is a time of growth, labor, and maturation. During this time, seeds planted in the spring grow and mature at this time.

Autumn is the time of harvest, a period when seeds planted in spring and grown in summer, ripen and are harvested. It is an exhilarating time as we reap what we have sown.

Winter is the season of closure, withdrawal, rest, and even death. It is when fields lie fallow and people withdraw from the bitter climate to rest. Invariably, another spring eventually comes, and the cycle begins again.

Plant the seed of hard work and trust the process,

In Living Your Best Life, you've got to first plant your seed of hard work, good things, and/or monetary investment. After this, you've got to trust the process because it may take some time for the external factors to manifest. But know that as your planting the right seeds internally, the external result will manifest, sooner or later. Trust the process. If you put in the work, if you sow the right seeds, the fruit is going to bear itself.

Start Living Your Best Life!

Throughout the course of this book, I have shown you that the best life is one that is achieved by striving to be your very best and functioning at your maximum capacity. It starts in your mind, and, even though it requires extremely hard work, the results are always rewarding and exhilarating. As you become your best, it is pertinent that you help others to become their best as well. You can do it!

Living Your Best Life is not about seeking to be perfect. It's seeking to make continuous progress! So, don't think you have to be perfect and do everything right; just seek to make progress continually. Seek to make improvements and get better. Be someone who keeps making progress, getting better and better as you continue to grow and mature.

Live your Best life… There's nothing or no one that can stop you being all that you were created to be and accomplishing the things in store for you—except you!

CHAPTER NINE: TRUE GOALS OF LIFE

It remains vital that you push through with every goal that you set in mind to achieve. Remember that planning and setting goals are important, and please, always refine your character so that you will turn out to be the best at what you do.

I wrote this book to encourage, equip and empower you to be your best self. I want to help you be all God has created you to be and reap the rewards of that. I also want to remind you that the best life won't be handed to you; you've got to work for it.

I encourage you to also grab a copy of my journal, *Winning: Living My Best Life Journal*. Use it as a tool to help you apply a lot of these things necessary to live their best life. The journal will help keep you on track.

> *Keep on asking, and you will receive what you ask for. Keep on seeking, and you will find. Keep on knocking, and the door will be opened to you. For everyone who asks, receives. Everyone who seeks, finds. And to everyone who knocks, the door will be opened.* -**Matthew 7:7-8**

> *Do to others whatever you would like them to do to you. This is the essence of all that is taught in the law are prophets.* -**Matthew 7:12**

> *A good tree produces good fruit, and a bad tree produces bad fruit. A good tree can't produce bad fruit, and a bad tree can't produce good fruit. So, every tree that does not produce good fruit is chopped down and thrown into the fire. Yes, just as you can identify a tree by its fruit, so you can identify people by their actions.* -**Matthew 7:17-20**

Chapter Ten

Quotes and Scriptures

You'll never change your life until you change something you do daily. The secret of your success is found in your daily routine.
-*John C. Maxwell*

Knowing is not enough; we must apply. Willing is not enough; we must do. -*Johann Wolfgang von Goethe*

We are what we repeatedly do. Excellence, then, is not an act, but a habit. -*Aristotle*

The successful person makes a habit of doing what the failing person doesn't like to do. -*Thomas Edison*

A dream becomes reality as a result of your actions, and your actions are controlled, to a large extent by your habits.
-*John Maxwell*

Depending on what they are, our habits will either make us or break us. We become what we repeatedly do. -*Stephen Covey*

Scripture Passages on Protection

But in that coming day no weapon turned against you will succeed. You will silence every voice raised up to accuse you.

These benefits are enjoyed by the servants of the Lord; their vindication will come from me. I, the Lord, have spoken!
-Isaiah 54:17

The Lord keeps you from all harm and watches over your life. The Lord keeps watch over you as you come and go, both now and forever. **-Psalm 121:7-8**

Scripture Passages on Being Fearless

So be strong and courageous! Do not be afraid and do not panic before them. For the Lord your God will personally go ahead of you. He will neither fail you nor abandon you.
-Deuteronomy 3:16

Don't be afraid, for I am with you. Don't be discouraged, for I am your God. I will strengthen you and help you. I will hold you up with my victorious right hand. **-Isaiah 41:10**

Scripture Passages on Wisdom

If you need wisdom, ask our generous God, and he will give it to you. He will not rebuke you for asking. **-James 1:5**

Get all the advice and instruction you can, so you will be wise the rest of your life. **-Proverbs 19:20**

For the Lord grants wisdom! From his mouth come knowledge and understanding. **-Proverbs 2:16**

Call to me, And I will answer you, and show you good and mighty things which you do not know. **-Jeremiah 33:3**

Come and listen to my counsel. I'll share my heart with you and make you wise. **-Proverbs 1:23**

CHAPTER TEN: QUOTES AND SCRIPTURES

Scripture Passages on Excellence

Whatever you do, work at it with all your heart, as working for the Lord, not for human masters. -**Colossians 3:23**

And you yourself must be an example to them by doing good works of every kind. Let everything you do reflect the integrity and seriousness of your teaching. -**Titus 2:7**

And may the Lord our God show us his approval and make our efforts successful. Yes, make our efforts successful! -**Psalms 90:17**

In the same way, let your light shine before others, that they may see your good deeds and glorify your Father in heaven.
-**Matthew 5:16**

Scripture Passages on Prosperity

And my God shall supply all your needs according to His riches and glory by Christ Jesus. -**Philippians 4:19**

But remember the Lord your God, for it is He who gives you the ability to produce wealth, and so confirms His covenant, which he swore to your ancestors, as it is today. -**Deuteronomy 8:18**

Give, and you will receive. Your gift will return to you in full— pressed down, shaken together to make room for more, running over, and poured into your lap. The amount you give will determine the amount you get back. -**Luke 6:38**

The Lord will send rain at the proper time from his rich treasury in the heavens and will bless all the work you do. You will lend to many nations, but you will never need to borrow from them. If you listen to these commands of the Lord your God that I am giving you today, and if you carefully obey them, the Lord will make you the head and not the tail, and you will always be on top and never at the bottom. You must not turn away from any of the commands I am giving you today, nor follow after other gods and worship them. -**Deuteronomy 28:12-16**

Scripture Passages on Healing

But he was pierced for our transgressions, he was crushed for our iniquities; the punishment that brought us peace was on him, and by his wounds we are healed. -**Isaiah 53:5**

*Praise the Lord, my soul, and forget not all his benefits—who forgives all your sins and heals all your diseases,
who redeems your life from the pit and crowns you with love and compassion.* -**Psalm 103:2-4**

Such a prayer offered in faith will heal the sick, and the Lord will make you well. And if you have committed any sins, you will be forgiven. -**James 5:15**

Scripture Passages on Direction

Trust in the Lord with all your heart;do not depend on your own understanding. Seek his will in all you do, and he will show you which path to take. -**Proverbs 3:5-6**

You are my hiding place; you will protect me from trouble and surround me with songs of deliverance.

I will instruct you and teach you in the way you should go; I will counsel you with my loving eye on you. -**Psalm 32:7-8**

The Lord directs the steps of the godly. He delights in every detail of their lives. -**Psalm 37:23**

About the Author

Howard Douglas Austin II has a passion and desire to help others and share vital knowledge as a life coach. When he discovered writing as an opportunity to truly connect with people from all over the globe, he clung to it without a second thought.

He holds a BS in Finance from Southeastern Louisiana University and began working in the Healthcare industry when he was only twenty-one. In just three years, he successfully transformed a small-startup firm into a multi-million dollar revenue-generating company. He has also successfully managed other companies, which have amassed more than 25 million dollars in revenue at the time of this printing. Austin's journey to greatness has been anything but rosy, as he has experienced both successes and failures. Yet, he has been able to navigate through his failures to determine issues that affect productivity and devise strategies to solve them.

Armed with his vast experience, Austin seeks to help and encourage others to become the very best in their fields. He writes on personal and spiritual development, tailoring books specifically to positively impact others. Coaching is more than just a profession or a hobby to him—it is his purpose and passion.

www.ingramcontent.com/pod-product-compliance
Lightning Source LLC
Chambersburg PA
CBHW071314110426
42743CB00042B/1998